BIG GAME FISHING

BIG GAME FISHING

Trevor Housby

BLANDFORD PRESS

POOLE · DORSET

Series Editor: Jonathan Grimwood
Illustrations by: Anita Lawrence

First published in the U.K. 1985 by Blandford Press,
Link House, West Street, Poole, Dorset, BH15 1LL.

Copyright © 1985 Blandford Press Ltd

Distributed in the United States by
Sterling Publishing Co., Inc.,
2 Park Avenue, New York, N.Y. 10016.

British Library Cataloguing in Publication Data

Housby, Trevor
  Big game fishing.
  1. Big game fishing—Europe
  I. Title
  799.1'6   SH603

ISBN 0 7137 1606-1

Typeset by Megaron Typesetting, Bournemouth

Printed in Spain by Gryelmo, Bilbao

Contents

*Dedicated to the regional government of
the Azores, the Portuguese Tourist
Office, Francisco Van Uden of
Pescatur, Ponta Delgada with thanks.*

Introduction

During the past decade there has been a dramatic increase in the number of anglers prepared to travel in search of big fish. In European waters – which stretch from Portugal and its islands up to Northern Norway – there is now tremendous potential for the big fish hunter.

While many of our fish, such as giant skate, halibut or conger, may not be glamorous when compared to the great fish of Australia, Mexico or the Caribbean, they do provide anglers on a moderate budget with a chance to catch a big fish, and for this reason they are included in my book.

Sharks also play a vital part in the European angler's big fish list, and in this respect we are lucky. From the Atlantic Islands to Norway large shark of several species are there to be taken, and some of these are in the world record class. Indeed, a growing awareness of shark as a sporting species means that many more anglers are taking shark fishing very seriously, and as a result many large specimens are being taken.

Then there are the tunas – the mighty blue fin, the hard-hitting big eyed tuna and, occasionally, the yellow fin – all 'thrills a minute' fish worthy of inclusion in any book on big game fishing. And finally we have the marlin – both blue and white – and the mighty broadbill swordfish, a primeval creature that offers any angler the ultimate big fish challenge. All these fish (and more) are available in European waters.

I am often asked, 'If you were to choose one place in the world to fish, where would you go?' My answer is the Azores. Those nine magnificent Atlantic Islands produce some of the greatest sport fishing in the world. Reachable by scheduled flights from practically every major airport, the Azores and their fishing are a must for the big game angler.

Trevor Housby
Hampshire

Broadbill Fishing

The broadbill swordfish is without doubt the world's most sought-after big game fish. Once thought to be extremely rare, the broadbill is now known to be common in most oceans of the world. By nature a secretive creature which lives and feeds at depths in excess of 900 feet, it will very occasionally surface to bask in the sun but under these circumstances can rarely be inticed to take a bait. Broadbill can reach weights of over 550 pounds although most rod-caught specimens weigh between two and four hundred pounds.

In European waters broadbill can be regarded as comparatively common off Southern Ireland and off the continental shelf. Broadbill have also been fished commercially for many years off Scotland, but the finest of all European broadbill grounds are located round the islands of the Azores and, to a lesser extent, Madeira.

At one time, Sesimbra, a fishing port on the Bay of Setubal in mainland Portugal was regarded as the finest broadbill area in the world. And during the 1950s and 1960s many, many anglers came from all over the globe to test their luck with this great fish. Many were unlucky – but most came away with a broadbill story to tell.

Tackle

Rods

The broadbill swordfish is a big, exceptionally strong creature which requires the heaviest of tackle. Most experienced anglers use a rod with an IGFA rating of 130 pounds. A few big game fishermen use rods of 80 pounds but none use anything lighter.

Reels

As most broadbill swordfish are fished for at exceptional depths a large reel is essential. 130 pound class Tournament reels can be used, but many anglers – myself included – prefer to use a star drag reel of the Penn Senator type. My choice is the 14-0 model but I know many broadbill fishermen who prefer the huge 16-0 size reel.

The Penn Senator reel range has a number of advantages.
1. The reels are extremely rugged.
2. The star drag system, although old fashioned, is simple and very reliable.
3. The 14-0 and 16-0 sized Senators hold a thousand plus yards of 130 class line.

Ample line capacity is essential, as most broadbill are hooked and fight at depths in excess of 750 feet; and with this amount of line already out it is absolutely essential to have plenty of line left on the reel drum.

Hooks and Traces

Like marlin, broadbill can be fished for with a trace made from commercial 'long line' nylon. At one time I used only wire as trace material but, in recent years, have come to realise that a bait presented on nylon often fishes better than one presented on wire. This is particularly true when livebaits are used.

The favoured line bait in Portuguese waters is rays bream, a deep-water fish which does not suffer from pressure change. Rays bream can be brought to the surface, put on a big hook and then lowered down into 900 plus feet of water without suffering damage from pressure. This is vital, for broadbill like to take live fish and a rays bream presented on a nylon trace will swim and act as a natural fish. Put that same bait on a wire trace and the stiffness of even braided wire will hamper the free-swimming movement of the bait. More important still, if – as often occurs – the bait swims over and round a nylon trace, the resulting tangle will not cause the trace to part should a broadbill pick up the bait. Should a similar tangle occur with a wire trace, the trace will usually snap as soon as the broadbill begins to move off with the bait.

Location and Methods

Light Sticks

In recent seasons broadbill swordfish have been caught in ever-increasing quantities using a combination of a natural bait illuminated by a chemical light stick. These light sticks were originally used as 'flames' in life rafts, and are made up as a sealed hollow tube containing two separate chemicals. When the stick is bent so that the two chemicals intermingle, the light stick turns into a powerful fluorescent flame which shines out through the container.

The technique for catching broadbill is to insert the light stick into the body of a large squid (see Fig. 1), so that the chemical light causes the squid to glow in the dark water. Alternatively, the light stick can be tied to the line directly above a dead fish. Both these illuminated-bait methods have proved to be extremely effective, and have now accounted for a great many swordfish.

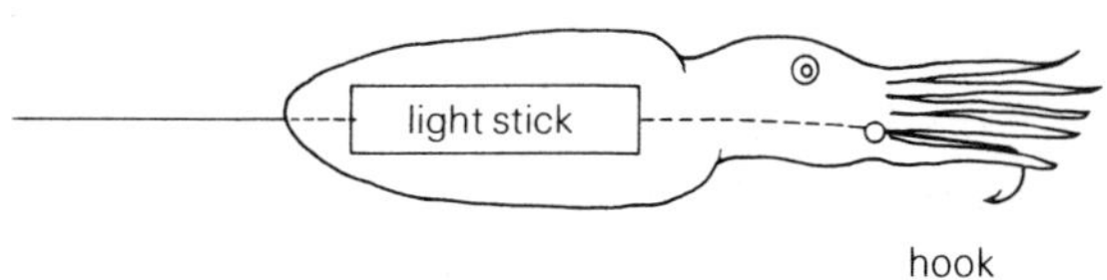

FIGURE 1   A chemical 'light stick' inserted into a large squid and fished deep is the most effective bait for broadbill.

Under normal circumstances illuminated bait are fished at depths in excess of 600 feet. Many boats use this method at night.

Although broadbill swordfish will occasionally strike at trolled artificial lures, few European anglers use this method. I personally know of only one broadbill caught in this way from a European port, and that fish, weighing close to 220 pounds, was taken off San Miguel, Azores on a trolled bait intended for tuna.

Livebait fishing is the preferred and proved method for catching broadbill. This technique was initially developed by José Braz of Sesimbra, Portugal. During the 1950s and early 1960s, when large broadbill were common off this section of the Portuguese coast, deep fishing with live rays bream produced a vast number of great fish and even more big-fish stories!

In those days anglers sailed out to the swordfish grounds on a conventional fishing boat, and then disembarked onto a tiny rowing boat called an *aiola*. Local fishermen rowed constantly to keep these tiny boats in position on the edge of the swordfish banks, and many an epic battle was fought from within the confines of such a boat. The livebait used consisted of the hardy rays bream, caught during the night and kept as live bait.

Then, as now, there was something pre-historic about the broadbill that fascinated anglers. Large eyes, leathery skin and stiff fins give this fish the appearance of a fearsome monster from the deep. To some extent the swordfish lives up to this sinister image, much of its life being spent at vast depths. Most of my fishing for swordfish has been done off the coasts of Portugal. As I have mentioned, at one time the underwater banks in the Bay of Setubal were one of the world's broadbill hotspots and anglers from Europe and many other parts of the world flocked to the lovely town of Sesimbra to fish for – and hopefully catch – a mighty broadbill.

Some were successful – but many failed – for broadbill as a species are totally unpredictable and often refuse to feed despite near perfect conditions. Unlike nearly every other species of big game fish, no two broadbill strikes are ever the same, and it takes a good angler to interpret and react to each individual bite.

One of the strangest takes I ever had was on one of those perfect Portuguese days when the sea is as flat as a millpond and the boatman does not have to work too hard to keep his position over the deep-sunk banks. We had been fishing since just after dawn, my bait was still fresh and lively after nearly four hours of fishing and I had every hope of an imminent strike. Two hundred yards away a commercial fishing boat was working with long lines and this is always a good sign, for hundreds of hooked and struggling fish act as a natural attraction for hunting swordfish.

As always, the strike came without warning. One second nothing, the next the rod lunged downward as somewhere – 600 feet below our keel – a swordfish smashed at the livebait with its formidable bill. Instantly I put the reel into free spool, to allow the bait fish to sink naturally. Strategically, this is vital for if a bait does not behave normally, the cautious swordfish will immediately vacate the danger area at high speed, spoiling any chance of catching a fish.

With the reel spool turning slowly, I hunched up over the rod and began the heart-stopping wait for the fish to turn, mouth and finally suck in the bait: more often than not this waiting is in vain. Swordfish seem to have a natural ability to sense danger and, as the seconds ticked away, I began to wonder if this was going to be yet another failure. Then, just over sixty seconds after the fish had struck the livebait with its bill, I sensed rather than felt a gradual tightening of the line.

Eyes fixed to where the heavy line entered the sea, I saw my line begin to move slowly against the tide and knew that the broadbill had my big bait in its bird-like jaw. Gradually the fish began to speed up and, as it did so, I pushed the reel lever into the 'lock up' position. Striking at this stage was out of the question. The fish was now close to a thousand feet below our keel and I knew that the current would have created a great bag in the line.

The trick is to wait for the fish to straighten out the bow in the line then, when the full weight of the running broadbill starts to pull the rod tip down, strike hard in the hope of setting the hook. I say *hope* for hooking a broadbill is never easy. Possibly 80 percent of broadbill strikes fail to produce a fish: of the other 20 percent at least half result in foulhooked fish, while a further 5 percent – half of the well-hooked fish – are lost during the course of the battle. At best broadbill is a chance game and undoubtedly the 'lost fish factor' adds to the sporting appeal of this great fish.

Most broadbill anglers are under a spell cast by their quarry and some are so badly afflicted by broadbill fever that they never bother with any other species. Still, at this stage of the battle, I did not have the time or inclination to worry about hooking percentages. The fish so far below me had obviously taken my bait and was now moving away at a steady speed. Then weight was suddenly on the rod in that lunge of power that only a broadbill can give. The moment my rod pulled over, I took several quick turns of the reel handle and leaned back to drive the hook home.

Normally I would have repeated the 'wind and strike' routine several times to make certain of the hook hold. With this fish, however, I did not need to follow the normal procedure. The moment I struck I felt the fish roll and plunge, and I knew for certain that it was well hooked, probably far back in the softer part of the mouth.

All billfish turn on the power when they feel a hook for the first time but this one went crazy. Within seconds the big reel was smoking, its line pouring off the spool at staggering speed. All I could do was hang on and let the huge fish run under full pressure. I knew it could not keep up its speed for too long: the spring of the rod and the heavy reel drag being bound to slow it down eventually. From my memory of the half-empty spool I estimate that that took close to 200 yards before slowing down to circle wide, deep down round the boat.

Behind me I could hear the boatman swinging the oars to keep the tiny boat pointed at the circling fish. All Portuguese fishermen talk to big fish and this one kept up a stream of invective, mostly about the parentage or otherwise of the big fish on the end of my line. Once settled into a circling routine, the big broadbill fought on at a steady pace. For over thirty minutes it was content to cruise but, from other battles, I knew that, sooner or later, it would lose its temper. Because of this I resisted the temptation to increase reel drag. Put too much drag on a green fish and a broken line is a certainty.

When the fish eventually did wake up it did so with a vengeance, rolling and plunging at high speed. Each time it attempted to dive I was pulled half out of my seat, and each time this happened I felt the boatman grab for my harness to stop me from going overboard. The first hour was now gone and the fish showed no sign of weakening. This did not surprise me. I once saw a German angler hook a broadbill at nine in the morning and lose it just after six in the evening. I felt good, and if the fight were to last all day I felt I was in good-enough shape to take any punishment the fish could hand out.

At the end of the second hour the fish suddenly changed tactics. For the first time it showed an inclination to give ground and in less than fifteen minutes I gained an estimated hundred yards of line, then I lost contact. Shortly before the line slackened the fish made a great lunge, and then the weight came off the line.

Both the boatman and I thought the hook hold had given way. So cursing our luck I started to wind up the slack line. When over half the line was back on the reel I slowly realised that the angle of the line was wrong. Instead of hanging straight down it ran out at an angle from the boat. The fish was still on and had risen almost to surface level.

A big broadbill on the surface is usually an unmistakable sight, with its great dorsal and fine upper-tail lobe showing clearly. The unnerving thing with this one was that when the great fish broke the surface only the dorsal fin showed. Worse still, the fish looked weak. Its great bill barely moved from side to side and it was obvious that something was seriously wrong. The truth became terribly apparent as we neared the stricken fish. The whole tail section had been chopped away by a shark. Only one European shark would tackle a large broadbill, so the culprit had to be a mako. The heavy jolt I had felt just before the fish began to rise must have been caused when the shark hit the billfish.

For me it was a tragedy: for my boatman just a slight

inconvenience. The best part of the fish was left and this would still fetch him good money in the Sesimbra market.

The odd thing about big fish – which any fisherman will tell you – is that you remember the ones you lose far longer than those that you catch. This poor mutilated fish has stuck in my mind for over 20 years. The remaining section was never weighed but if that fish had been intact I know it would have been a fine example of a broadbill.

Halibut Fishing

Never a common species, the halibut is also severely restricted in range. And yet despite this – and its general rarity – the halibut is a popular target fish for European anglers, in particular for the big game specialists from Northern Europe.

Essentially a cold-water species and technically a flatfish, halibut are sometimes found off the coast of Norway but are more common round Orkney, Shetland and the Faroe Islands. Of the three localities it is Orkney that seems to produce the most and largest rod-and-line caught halibut. Halibut grow to a huge size and commercial fishing records indicate that halibut can reach weights in excess of 400 pounds – the largest reported fish weighing 625 pounds when gutted. The rod-caught record now stands at over 200 pounds.

As a fighting species the halibut is a powerful active fish that puts up a tremendous battle when hooked. The fish's fighting ability is accentuated by its love of fast tidal areas, where its strength and body shape can be used to maximum advantage.

Tackle

Rods

Light tackle and halibut do not mix as the fish is a rough-and-tumble fighter with a lot of points in its favour. Most experienced halibut fishermen use 80-pound IGFA class rods, and tackle should be selected very carefully indeed. A shoulder harness and a rod-rest of the groin-protector type must be used as halibut can be very fierce fighters.

Reels

The most popular halibut reel, and the most successful, is the British-made Tatler V. This multiplier-type of reel was used to catch the European-record halibut, of 234 pounds caught by Mr Colin Booth. Penn Senator reels are also popular – the high speed 6-0 version being perfect for halibut fishing. At least 400 yards of line should be wound onto the reel.

Lines

For use in a heavy flow-tide I find that a dacron line (polyester fibre) is best. The disadvantage of dacron is its lack of elasticity and its tendency to fray if scraped across an underwater obstruction. However, its advantage is that it is thinner than nylon of similar breaking-strain and it cuts readily through the tidal flows so loved by halibut, allowing the angler to fish more comfortably.

Hooks

Even a comparatively small halibut has a huge mouth, and large hooks are an essential part of the halibut angler's armoury. The best hooks for this work are Mustad Seamaster hooks, size 8-0 or 10-0. If possible, avoid the American-style beak hooks (see Fig. 2). These, in my experience, tend to be brittle and may well break during a prolonged battle. Halibut are never a common fish, and to hook and then lose a fish due to tackle failure is inexcusable as well as being bitterly disappointing.

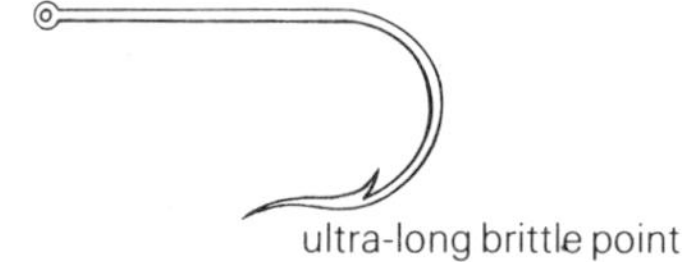

FIGURE 2   An American-style beak hook. These are often brittle and have a tendency to break.

All hooks should be sharpened before use, and the hook should be checked regularly during a day's fishing and resharpened if necessary.

Traces and Swivels

A hooked halibut will almost certainly apply a considerable amount of pressure to both the line and the actual trace. For this reason, trace material should be chosen carefully.

Many anglers use nylon-covered wire for trace material, others pin their faith on 'long line' nylon. Of these two materials I prefer the nylon, as nylon-covered wire has a tendency to absorb water. This in turn sets up a corrosive action, eating into the inner core. Often this damage is minute, but it is usually enough to cause the trace to snap and yet another 'giant halibut escapes' story is born.

Anglers who quite happily spend vast amounts of money on a rod and reel often penny-pinch when it comes to hooks, traces and swivels. This is obviously idiotic. A hook and trace have to absorb a tremendous amount of punishment and should be made up from the best materials available.

I like to use a trace six or seven feet long for halibut, constructed in two equal lengths, joined by a central barrel swivel (see Fig. 3). This central swivel helps to prevent the trace from twisting during use. The best swivels for this job are the Berkeley 5-0 swivels. When using 'long line' nylon I use two crimps to secure the swivel or hook (see Fig. 4). This makes a strong, neat join which is capable of withstanding great pressure. I find that nylon of 150 or 200 pounds breaking strain is perfect for this style of trace.

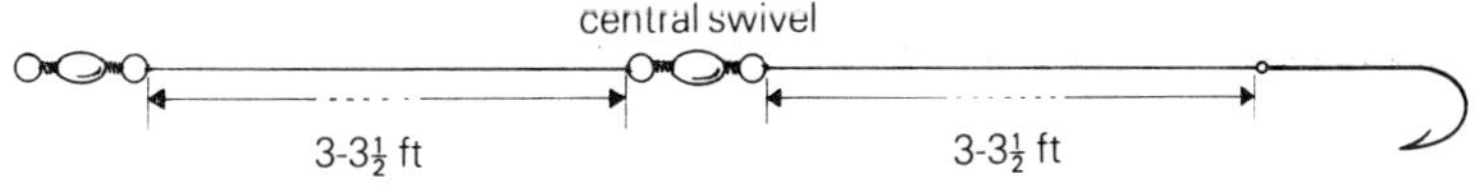

FIGURE 3   A central barrel swivel is used to join two lengths of 150/200 pound 'long line' nylon to make a strong trace. Halibut traces need to be made from the best materials available.

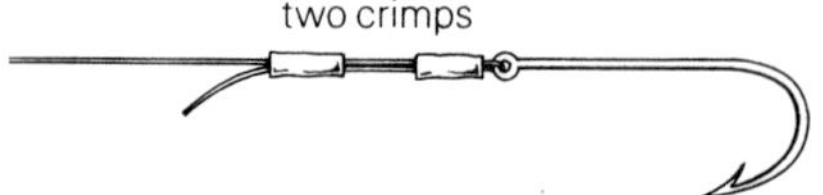

FIGURE 4   Crimps can be used to secure a hook or swivel to 'long line' nylon.

Lures

Halibut are predatory fish, that fall regularly to artificial lures which simulate natural fish. The most useful lure for this work is a large pirk (see Fig. 5). A pirk is simply a heavily chromed metal bar, bent to an angle that makes it move and flutter when worked through the water.

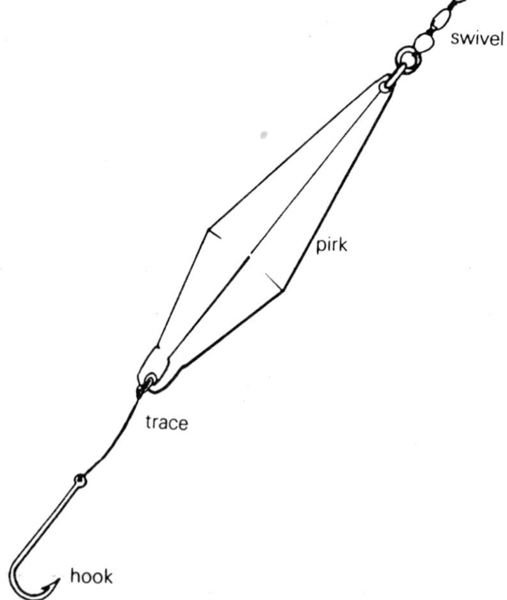

FIGURE 5   A large pirk lure of the type ideal for catching halibut.

Pirk-type lures are easily made at home from lengths of lead-filled chrome tubing of the type used on old office chairs, etc. The end of the tube is first flattened off and drilled, then the tube is filled with molten lead. Hooks can then be fitted via a split ring or by using a heavy-duty trace.

Location and Methods

I have only fished halibut in two areas. Rathin Island off the coast of Northern Ireland and in waters off the Orkneys. Of the two localities Orkney has produced most fish, up to and including the current British and European record for the species.

As I have said, halibut are a strong, active and highly predatory species which show a great liking for heavy tide flows. And the Pentland Firth between mainland Scotland and the Orkneys is a perfect example of the preferred halibut habitat. The whole of the firth is a savage *maelstrom* of heavy tides and overfall areas, created by the upthrust of water deflected from submerged reef formations. Fishing the firth is never easy; anchoring is virtually impossible; and most of the fishing is done on the drift.

The majority of halibut are hooked by accident on tackle intended for cod and ling. Most of these fish break free in the first few minutes of battle. While a few, mostly the smaller fish, are successfully played out and boated, almost all such halibut are taken soon after a small coalfish or codling has taken the baited hook. Of the two species, coalfish seem to be the most attractive to hunting halibut. I find that giant skate also fall readily to whole or filleted coalfish, so presumably the coalfish has an inbuilt scent that the giant fish of the Northern seas find particularly attractive.

Coalfish as bait catch far more big fish than the normally-attractive and oily mackerel, and whenever possible I use coalfish in preference to any other bait. Unfortunately my successes boating halibut have been extremely limited. My experiences, on the other hand, have been very full indeed!

I remember particularly well one trip from Stromness. The intention was to fish off Marwick Head and our target, as always, was a giant halibut. First stop was a wreck inside Hoy Island, a place where small coalfish could often be taken six at a time on brightly-coloured mackerel feathers. For some strange reason the fish were totally off food that day and after thirty minutes only one diminutive coalfish had been brought aboard. To continue here was obviously a waste of time, so we moved off to a new mark close under Hoy Island where our luck changed and the coalfish were plentiful.

In less than ten minutes we half filled a bait box and then, not wishing to destroy further fish stocks, we headed directly for our drift area off Marwick Head. With the heavy rods made up and special pirk-type lures attached, we baited the big trailing hooks with either whole or cut coalfish according to our personal preferences. The weather was beautifully clear and bright, with a warm sun and hardly any breeze to ruffle the normally turbulent sea. And inshore of us the lovely island stood out in clear detail to reveal a stunning view of the wild, rugged coastline.

I had cut my coalfish up from the tail to a point just behind the head, I had then removed the backbone to leave two flapping fillets of flesh joined by the head of the bait. I always use this method when I employ coalfish as bait. My theory being that the joined fillets give what is normally a stiff bait the opportunity to move attractively below the large chromed pirk lure.

Once our skipper had lined up his shore marks, so that we would be fishing a known halibut drift, we went to work. The sea bed round Orkney seems to consist of a jumble of jagged rocks and upthrust reefs. Tackle losses are inevitably high over such ground and I was grateful that I was using home-made pirks rather than expensive shop-bought lures. At the end of an hour I had lost two sets of terminal tackle, a companion had lost no less than five sets of gear and – apart from a 12 pound ling – we had not caught anything at all.

With my third bait of the day down close to sea-bed level, I began to work my rod tip up and down to make the pirk and bait flutter and dance temptingly over the bottom. When the bite did come it felt exactly as though I had once again fouled some underwater obstruction. My rod slowly dragged round and down as I cursed the prospect of losing yet another set of tackle. In a last, annoyed attempt to pull free of the snag I heaved hard back on the rod and instantly realised that I was into a fish.

Like all big halibut this one reacted savagely, turning down tide at high speed. Using its huge lozenge-shaped body as a drogue, the fish took line fast then turned and kited across the tide in typical hard-fighting fashion. I knew instinctively that this fish was a big one. Few Orkney halibut weigh less than a 100 pounds, many being closer to the 200-pound mark but at this stage it was impossible to estimate the weight.

The trick with halibut is to fight them hard. I like to keep the fish's head up, continually winding and pumping to keep the fish coming towards the surface. Even this can be dangerous. Halibut have a habit of taking a sudden unexpected nose dive, which can easily smash a line if the angler is not fully ready to slacken his reel drag the second the hooked fish starts to go down. This fish fought well but without a great deal of style. Twice it changed direction and on both occasions took a few yards of line off the big reel.

Finally, however, it started to come steadily up and the skipper and crew started to stand by with their gaffs. The tide was raging by this time and I knew that once the fish surfaced we had only a matter of seconds to set the gaffs firmly. Slowly I gained more line until the halibut swam into sight, well below the surface and a few yards behind the boat. By anyone's standards the fish was huge. I have seen some good halibut caught but never had I seen one that looked as big as this. Raising it to surface level was easy as the fish seemed tired and came up without fuss.

It surfaced and we suddenly saw, to our horror, that the big hook was hanging from its mighty jaw by one thin sliver of translucent skin. I knew at once that I had a slim chance of boating the fish. If only I could inch it forward into gaffing range, then the battle was won . . . but the halibut thought otherwise. . . .

Instead of staying dormant for those few crucial seconds, it swung its body sideways tearing out the big hook instantly. My huge pirk bait was actually thrown high into the air as the fish moved and stunned we all stood and watched silently as the giant fish vanished into the tide-ripped waters below the boat.

Halibut often take a bait when least expected, as happened on one occasion while fishing the Tritor Bank off St

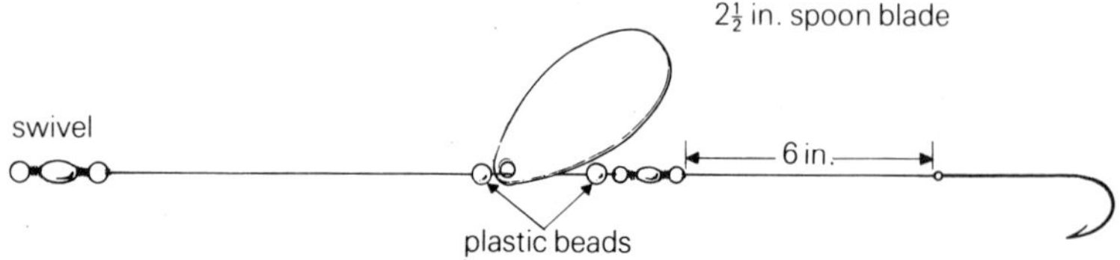

FIGURE 6   Simple attractor spoon, used in front of a natural bait to add flash. The spoon is held in place by two plastic beads.

Margaret's Hope, Orkney. I was after cod and ling using a simple attractor spoon rig, baited with a slice of fresh mackerel (see Fig. 6). The Tritor Bank is a deep, tide washed patch of sand and gravel which is only fishable at a certain state of the tide. Cod are particularly common on this bank. Not big fish, but useful 8 and 10 pound cod which provide first class fishing on 30 pound class tackle.

On this day I had already taken a dozen cod and two or three ling of 10/12 pounds in weight. With the tide slackening our prospects were good and the boat crew – ever hopeful for additional market money – insisted that sport could only get better as the tide continued to slacken.

Cod of any size are voracious fish which take a bait solidly in distinctive style. And when the halibut took, its bite also seemed typically cod like! A double rap on the rod tip, followed by a heavy pull that dragged the tip slowly down towards the sea. I was so convinced that a cod was the culprit I remember telling the skipper to get a small gaff ready.

Still thinking medium-sized cod, I set the hook and started to crank the handle of my Tatler reel. Under normal circumstances the fish should have lifted easily, kiting upwards at the first sign of rod pressure. This fish did not move for my rod, if anything it felt like hooking the sea bed: a solid unmoving mass that felt totally lifeless. For several seconds my rod remained motionless, and then I became aware of a slight nodding movement of the rod tip. The movement suddenly turned into a savage jerk which set the big reel screaming as a very large, very live fish turned and tore off down tide.

This sudden lunge took everyone by surprise but luckily the

reel clutch was only set for medium-weight cod. If it had been turned right up, the line would have parted instantly but instead it gave line easily, allowing the fish to move against light drag pressure. This saved the day. As the fish continued to run I began to tighten the star drag until the fish was pulling out line under twenty pounds of reel drag. The effect was dramatic, instead of simply cruising over the sea bed the fish took off at high speed, obviously alarmed by the sudden drag. I think it was at this stage we all realised that the fish was a halibut. No other species in Orcadian waters would fight in this style, not even a giant skate. The problem facing us was that we also realised our chances of landing this fish were slim: halibut and 30 pound tackle do not go together.

Despite this I was determined to do my best for I have taken a good many big fish on comparatively light tackle, and felt that given time I had a fighting chance of boating this one. To a degree luck was already on my side. I had hooked the halibut on a slackening tide and I still had the whole of the slack tide period to get it aboard. If I hadn't landed it before the tide began to flood I would lose the fish, for full tide on the Triton is a fearful rush of water. The skipper sensing my need to get above the fish buoyed the anchor for later recovery and – by judicious use of his engine – placed the boat directly above the wildly fighting fish.

The fight soon became a pump and wind affair, with both sides giving and gaining line. Twice I had the fish up to mid-water and on both occasions it turned, then ripped off enough line to regain the sea bed. Fortunately halibut seldom adopt skate tactics and try to hug the bottom, instead they keep on the move, relying on bulk and strength to wear down their adversary.

I can vividly remember many things that I saw during this battle. At one stage I was looking directly towards the village of Longhope, which only a year before had lost most of its men in a tragic, yet incredibly heroic lifeboat accident. Still later, I watched the despondent plight of a solitary tern being hunted down by a pair of vicious arctic skuas. Time and again the little sea bird eluded the sea hawks, only to fall at the last to their combined effort. When the little sea swallow died I knew I was going to beat that fish. Maybe I sensed a weakening.

Whatever the reason, I began to pile on the pressure and the great fish began to come up.

The first sight of a big halibut is something that no sea angler can forget. A great diamond-shaped creature, pale and primeval, rising slowly to the surface. The crew – all experienced long-line fishermen – knew exactly how to boat a big halibut. And with two gaffs firmly planted, the fish was dragged inboard. Even then the battle was not finished. The halibut went into a final frenzy, smashing an engine box to matchwood before finally laying quiet. Back at St Margaret's Hope it weighed in at 106½ pounds. By halibut standards a small fish, but by my standards of a good fight, a great catch and one I shall never forget.

Marlin Fishing

Although normally regarded as a warm water species, blue marlin do penetrate in fairly reasonable numbers to European waters and very occasionally stragglers have been reported from as far north as Norway.

For sport-fishing purposes, however, the islands of the Canaries, Madeira and the Azores offer the greatest potential to big game anglers. In recent seasons the Madeira islands have produced increasing numbers of very large blue marlin. Individual specimens to over 1,000 pounds have been taken and the average weight of fish taken currently exceeds 500 pounds. Even by Caribbean standards, the Madeira-caught fish are of outstanding size and, at present, Madeira leads against other European centres as the marlin-fishing hotspot.

During 1983, however, a number of large blue marlin began to be hooked, landed or lost adjacent to the island of San Miguel, in the Azores archipelago. At present this area has hardly been explored as a source of these fish, but the most recent catches indicate that, in time, the Azores like Madeira could become a marlin paradise.

Marlin are fascinating fish – nomadic wanderers – who tend to swim and feed as individuals. Sometimes, when shoals of bait fish are plentiful, a number of separate blue marlin may be found feeding in one comparatively small area, but at no time do these fish shoal. The bait-fish shoals are simply a common factor which has attracted and condensed the ever hungry, always hunting marlin. Marlin are not selective feeders, although certain types of fish attract them more than others. Bonito, dorado (dolphin) and squid make up their main food supply but marlin will also hunt mackerel and any other fish of takable size which come their way. I was once present when the stomach contents of a 420 pound blue marlin were being examined. Inside the bag of the stomach was a complete, but partially digested, white marlin measuring 72 inches in length. Proof that a hungry blue marlin is capable of eating fish of considerable size.

Most rod-caught blue marlin are taken on natural or artificial baits, trolled at surface level. Because of this many anglers regard the marlin as a surface feeder. This is only partially true. The marlin is an opportunist. If food fish shoals swim near the surface then that is where the marlin will feed: if the same food fish decide to swim deep, then the marlin will follow them down.

Many boat skippers and anglers do not take this into account, and continue unsuccessfully to troll baits at surface level when the fish are feeding hundreds of feet beneath the surface of the sea. However, experienced marlin fishermen look for certain signs, something to show just where marlin are most likely to be found feeding.

For example, a raft of floating weed or sea-borne flotsam will often offer tiny shoal fish a temporary shelter. Dorado know this and recognise the weed rafts as a place to find a plentiful food supply. The dorado are then preyed upon, in turn, by blue marlin, which are hunted by the anglers. This is just a simple example of why it makes sense to fish round or close to floating weed, etc. A second example of a likely sign is when a concentration of flying fish are located. These beautiful, active little fish are another favoured food of dorado and bonito, both favoured food of the marlin tribe.

On days when there are no obvious signs to follow and several hours of trolling have produced no strikes on the surface, the answer is to switch to drift fishing, using live mackerel or small bonito, fished very deep.

Tackle

Huge marlin have been caught on 30 pound and 50 pound IGFA-class rods, using light reels to match. But far more marlin have been lost on such tackle. For this reason my advice is to fish heavy and boat rather than lose a blue marlin you hook.

Rods

80 or 130 pound IGFA-class rods should be used for blue marlin fishing in European waters. Many such rods are available, mostly of American origin, although Hardy of Alnwick, in England, make a fine range of big game rods. All big game rods for marlin should be fitted with a full set of roller guides. The best are manufactured by the Tycoon Tackle, Mildrun or AFTCO companies in America. Never be tempted to purchase a rod which has poor-quality rod rings (guides), even though there are many cheap guides on the market which are of inferior design and poor quality. Stick to the known, tried and tested patterns and you will not go far wrong, to say nothing of standing a better chance of landing your fish.

Reels

Marlin are fast, active fighters that tend to spend much of their time on or above the surface. The ideal reel for this sort of battle is a multiplier which incorporates a lever drag system The best and most popular models belong to the Penn International range. Penn produce reels for specific line-class work, *i.e.* International 12, 20, 30, 50, 80 and 130 class. The idea is that the reel and line can be matched to a specific weight of rod. For marlin 80 or 130 class are ideal.

Other reels to consider are Everoll (Italy), Fin-Nor (USA) and Hardy Zane Grey (England). Both the Hardy and the Fin-Nor are very expensive but very high quality products.

Lines

Few big game anglers can agree on what type of line to use for marlin. At one time dacron (polyester fibre) line was regarded as the standard line to use for all big game fishing. In recent seasons, however, dacron has rather fallen from favour.

The chief argument against dacron is that it has little or no elasticity, which means that when the line is under full tension during a battle it may part if touched by another fish or if it comes into contact with anything rough. This criticism is valid, and it is always a bitter blow to lose a good fish but, as always, there are two sides to the story.

Dacron, due to its lack of stretch is perfect as a trolling line. When a big fish hits a bait travelling at speed behind a boat, a line such as nylon – which has a tremendous natural elasticity – may cushion the blow, masking penetration of the hook on initial impact. This does not occur with dacron, when most fish are hooked on hitting the bait.

Many top anglers and charter boat captains who switched to nylon lines a few years ago are now beginning to turn back to dacron, simply because of its much-better hooking power. Personally, I think there is a place for both dacron and nylon lines. Dacron for trolling with natural or artificial lures; nylon for drift fishing with live or deadbait.

For those who prefer to use nylon, my advice is to choose and use the fully tried and tested makes. The favourite being 'Ande T' line monofilament. The T stands for 'tournament line', showing that this particular type can be used in tournaments fished to IGFA rules.

Traces

Bill fish do not have teeth so wire traces are not essential. Most experienced marlin anglers prefer to use Japanese 'long line' monofilament which has a breaking strain of approximately 400 pounds. It also has a very durable finish which is strong enough to withstand the normal chaffing that occurs from the rough surface of a marlin's bill or lips. Nylon traces of this type are perfect for trolling.

Some anglers prefer to fish with wire. The only reason for this being the ever-possible chance of a big shark picking up the bait. For if a nylon trace is used the shark may well bite through the trace long before it can be brought to the gaff.

Hooks

Flat forged 8-0, 10-0 or 12-0 needle-eyed hooks are best for trolling (see Fig. 7). For bait fishing, a hook with an offset

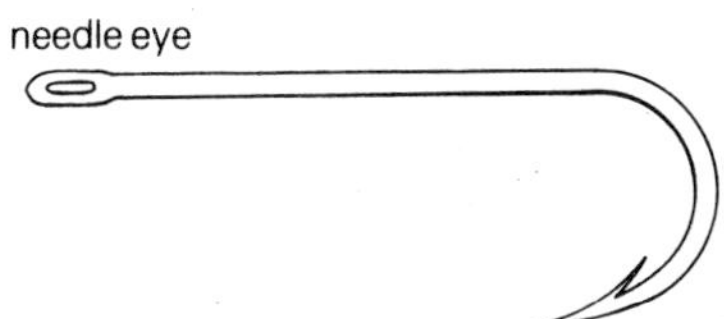

FIGURE 7 Use a flat forged needle-eyed hook when trolling for blue marlin as these are strong and reliable.

point is preferable, the best pattern available being the Mustad Seamaster.

Swivels

Only the best makes of swivel should be used for all aspects of big game fishing. The Berkeley Company of America market a fine range of reasonably-priced barrel swivels. These are simple yet highly efficient, offering strength and reliability at low cost.

At the other end of the scale come the expensive patterns, such as the Sampo swivel. I have used both patterns and of the two I favour the Berkeley range.

The 5-0 size is perfect for all forms of big game fishing, and so far this pattern of swivel has never let me down.

Natural Baits

Blue marlin can be caught on a wide variety of natural baits, and in European waters these baits are mostly used alive. Livebaits can be fished deep from a drifting boat, or trolled very slowly behind a moving boat. This trolling with livebait can be very effective when a marlin has been sighted on the surface. Under these circumstances the bait should be trolled round the basking fish (see Fig. 8). Few marlin will refuse a livebait.

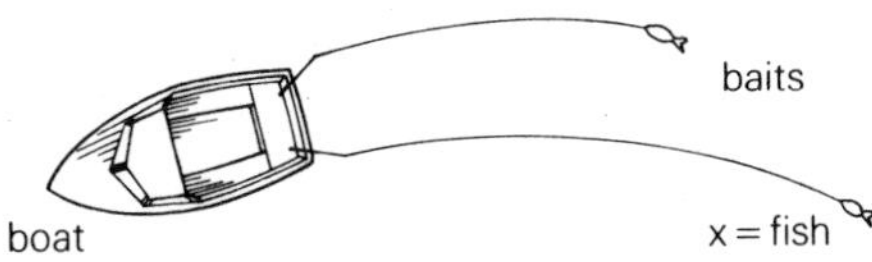

FIGURE 8 When marlin are basking on the surface a bait trolled around them is often a deadly form of fishing.

31

Live fish baits can be hooked in a variety of ways. The simplest is to use a two hook rig (see Fig. 9) so that the bait is attached by the lip only. Marlin are not stupid, and any natural bait that does not move in a lifelike manner will be ignored. For this reason, deadbaits should be trolled much faster than livebait.

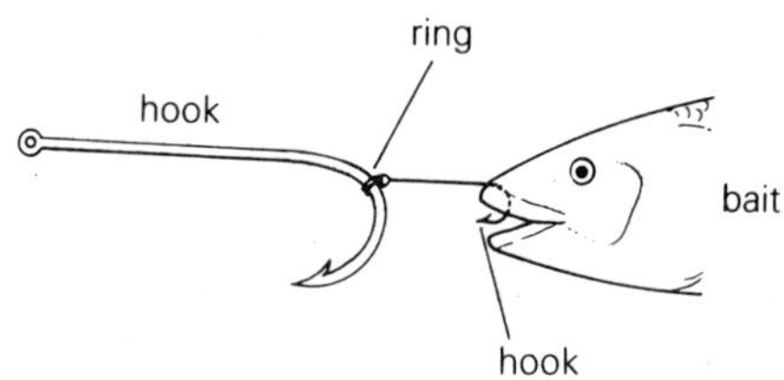

FIGURE 9   A double hook rig with the bait attached by the lip only is the most successful way of attaching a livebait.

Mullet, mackerel and small bonito make the best trolling baits. Mullet make particularly good baits as they are heavily-scaled fish which stand up well to being trolled at speed through water.

Artificial Baits

Marlin of all size will accept artificial lures. Some of the largest blue marlin ever caught have been taken on artificials. Nearly always on a Kona Head-type lure (see Fig. 10).

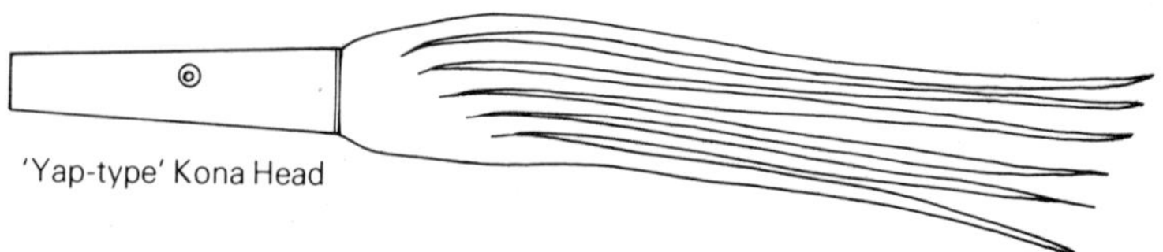

FIGURE 10   A 'Yap-type' Kona Head lure. Kona Heads – which are available in many colours and colour combinations – are the most effective artificial lures yet developed for marlin. They should be fished in the wake of a boat.

Originating from Hawaii, the Kona Head lures are manufactured extensively in America. Companies such as

Boone Baits and Yap Lures produce a wide variety of head shapes and lure colours. While these baits are not cheap they are essential for marlin fishing.

When choosing this type of bait it is necessary to take into account the natural colours of the bait fish found in the area you intend to fish. If bonito are the predominant bait-species then blue and white lures should be used. In an area where dorado are commonly encountered, then green and yellow lures should be selected. All-black lures can also produce fish. If squid are plentiful in a target area, then pink and black lures often work well. Under most circumstances, lures which incorporate yellow, blue, green or black fish best.

Obviously many such lures are created to catch anglers rather than marlin but, occasionally, a totally-outlandish lure will produce spectacular results: usually on one day only. We still have a great deal to learn about the feeding habits of marlin, and about what exactly triggers-off a feeding response to a totally unnatural colour. Light intensity undoubtedly has a great deal to do with this response but, as yet, it is impossible to link lighting conditions to colour patterns.

Using Deadbaits

Most natural baits are rigged to skip over the wave tops. To do this effectively the baits should be fished well astern of the boat and, if possible, outriggers used to keep the bait on the surface.

Marlin normally take a dead natural bait with caution so as soon as a bait is taken the angler must hold the rod and knock the reel out of gear. This allows the marlin to take the bait into its mouth and move off without hindrance. Striking a running fish is a matter of personal timing and previous experience. A confident fish is easy to hook. A cautious feeder, however, can present problems.

Normally a marlin will take the offered bait and move off at increasing speed. Under these circumstances the fish should be allowed to take 20 to 30 yards of line before the reel lever is pushed forward to engage the gears. The strike should be made the second the marlin's weight is felt on the rod. If – for one reason or another – the hook fails to engage, the marlin can sometimes be encouraged to strike again by rapidly cranking the reel handle to bring the bait splashing up to the surface. Once hooked, marlin react in a variety of ways. Some will expend their strength by continuously leaping or 'greyhounding' across the surface, while others will jump once and immediately sound to a great depth. Fish which do this are very difficult to play, far more difficult in fact than fish which stay on the surface.

Using Artificial Baits

Large blue marlin will often take an artificial bait within 10 to 15 yards of the boat, as it appears that the bubble and boil of the wake attracts hunting marlin. It is under these conditions that the artificial Kona Head-style lure produces the best results. To fish an artificial lure correctly, pre-set the drag of the reel to a known poundage. For example, on an 80 pound class outfit the reel drag is normally set to a strike drag of 25 to 28 pounds. Setting a reel drag is a two-person job. It is done by attaching the free end of the line to a spring balance, then adjusting the reel-drag setting until the reel just begins to give line at the required poundage.

Settings should be checked regularly as expansion and contraction of metal parts can seriously alter the original setting of a reel. This is most likely to occur when a reel is subjected to extremes of temperature.

Marlin usually come only once to an artificial bait. Obviously the moment a marlin closes its mouth over a plastic or acrylic lure it realises that it has made a serious mistake, and promptly tries to eject the suspect object. This is the reason why the lure should always be fished with the reel locked up to full strike drag.

From my own experiences of lure fishing it would appear that there is little that an angler can do to help set the hook. The fish either hits the bait and the hook is set on impact, or it hits the bait and the hook fails to penetrate. Fish lost on the take are very common, which is understandable when you make a close examination of the marlin's 'bird-like' mouth. Marlin may not have teeth but the mouth and lips of these fish are exceptionally hard, offering little hold for a big hook.

Despite the somewhat increased chance of lost fish, the use

of artificial lures is to be recommended. Artificials are easy to rig, clean to use and come in a wide range of colour combinations, to suit various conditions and situations. Most important still, a Kona Head-type lure will raise more fish than any other known marlin bait. Lures can obviously be designed and tuned to give a perfect action: they can also be customised to fit an angler's requirements. And many top marlin anglers automatically customise all their baits.

Some of these personalised lures are now produced commercially. There are rattle heads, which incorporate a loose ball inside the head; jet heads, which are drilled to send out enticing streams of bubbles as they are trolled through the water; and chug heads, which have the front end scooped out to throw a shower of spray as the bait bounces through the surface water. Most experienced anglers have their own particular fads about baits. Some theories produce little or nothing in the way of increased catches, whereas other modifications prove so successful that they are soon turned into standard patterns.

Marlin lures are not at all cheap and should be looked after carefully. Plastic or acrylic head material can chip or splinter when dropped on deck, while a damaged leading-edge can totally destroy the killing action of a lure. So make sure all such baits are handled with care.

Sometimes marlin strike at a lure without anyone noticing the strike. For this reason it pays to examine a lure regularly. When a marlin raps a lure it usually leaves a distinctive scrape mark (similar to that left by a file). If a bait is brought in, checked and found to have a new scrape mark, then it is worth turning the boat to recover the same area of sea. This may sound like a long shot but it is surprising how often it will pay off.

Location and Methods

All bill fish are large and dangerous. More than one angler, mate or skipper has been killed by a blue marlin, and I can cite two instances of marlin getting their own back on men and boats over the last two seasons.

In the first instance, a hooked fish weighing in at around 120 pounds went berserk ramming a big charter boat three times. The first time the fish struck, its bill went neatly through the side of the boat. The second time the beak angled up from close to the waterline splintering part of the deck. The third time the fish drove its beak right through the transom of the boat, snapping its bill off in the process.

Total damage to the boat was a little over £3,000, and all of this was caused by a *small* blue marlin. If a big 500 pound fish had been involved in the attack the boat would have suffered even greater damage and there might well have been a fatality.

In the second instance, the marlin weighed little more than a 100 pounds but had only been fighting for approximately 15 minutes when it was gaffed and was obviously green (*i.e.* very much alive). However, as the catch was made during a tournament when time mattered, the crew were prepared to get the fish into the boat as rapidly as possible. Unfortunately, the boat lurched as the struggling fish was hauled in over the side and the marlin's bill transfixed the mate's leg at a point just below his knee joint. This left the boat's skipper with the unenviable task of trying to club the marlin to death while, at the same time, trying to pull the bill free from the mate's leg. As luck would have it the whole operation was performed without further damage being inflicted. The mate was lucky. If the marlin had started to jump and thrash round, the mate's whole leg would certainly have been ripped apart. The injured man was soon ashore and apart from a nasty scar, he fully recovered. He was lucky, incredibly lucky. All big fish are dangerous and should be killed or released as quickly as possible, something I ensure whenever I fish.

During 1979 I was fortunate enough to win a major marlin tournament which was then regarded as the world championship. The tournament was a five-day event, and the winner was the angler who notched up the top number of points with each pound of fish taken being classed as one point scored.

On the first day I was off to a moderately good start, with a smallish fish weighing in at a little over 100 pounds. On this first day only a handful of fish were caught, one of which was mine, but a better fish was boated, which gave the lucky angler a little over 200 points lead on me.

The second day was equally poor for everyone. I did not even sight a fish and few boats weighed in. On the third day nothing much occurred for some hours, and most of us secretly expected yet another poor day's fishing. During a tournament, however, there is always a chance of a fish, and no angler can afford to relax his vigil. Fortunately for me I was standing beside one of my two rods when I saw a huge shadow appear directly astern of my frantically swimming Kona Head lure. The shadow turned into a big fish, which lit up, showing iridescent-blue markings almost as brilliant in colouring as neon light.

The fish was definitely interested but slightly uncertain about the plastic bait. Once the marlin faded away, only to re-appear seconds later. It certainly wanted that bait but something in the way the lure moved was obviously warning the great fish to take care. The only thing I could think of was to crank my reel handle rapidly so that the bait shot away from the big fish. My idea was to make the Kona Head simulate the frantic escape-behaviour of a terrified bait fish.

It worked. The huge marlin was suddenly convinced that a tasty meal was on the verge of escaping, and this time there was no hesitation. It headed straight for the apparently fleeing bait and, at little more than a trace length behind the boat, I saw the marlin's mouth open to suck in the lure. The second its jaws clamped over the bait I swept the rod out of its holder and struck hard to drive the hook point and barb solidly into the marlin's iron jaw.

I had obviously been successful for, as I frantically scrambled into the fighting chair, I was aware of a huge fish flinging itself high out of the water directly astern of the boat. This leap gave me just enough time to ram my rod butt into the gimbal of the fighting chair and then the fish took off at speed. I missed many of the marlin's spectacular jumps while snapping the fighting harness onto the lugs on my 80 class International reel.

I do remember, however, hearing the boat crew shout aloud at each jump, and the snarl of the rapidly-turning reel spool gave full indication of how far and fast the fish was travelling. With everything finally in position, I was able to pay more attention to the fish's spectacular display of aerobatics. By this stage, however, the mighty fish was over 200 yards away from the boat and breaking surface every few seconds. Only one fish – the mako shark – can out-jump a marlin and no mako I have ever hooked came out as fast, as high or as many times as this big blue did. Later the skipper told me he had counted thirty-two jumps on that first run. Most of this action I missed through paying attention to the reel and tackle.

With an estimated 250 to 300 yards of line already out, the fish changed tactics and began to dive. I did my utmost at this stage to stop the great fish from sounding. Large marlin often dive to incredible depths and then die, leaving the angler with a long slog trying to winch up a totally dead weight from a great depth.

Having been involved in several such unpleasant incidents I did my utmost to slow the fish down. Succeeding in my attempt at a depth of about 250 feet when the marlin eventually decided to head back to fight a surface battle for survival. From the changing angle of the line I was aware of its action, and cranked the reel handle at top speed to keep my line tight on the rising fish.

This time when the marlin came through the surface it put on a magnificent display of temper, leaping and thrashing in one small area where the water was soon whipped up to a fine, white foam. Although I had stopped the fish from diving, it was still full of life and ready to fight. Even so, we decided to try to regain some line by backing the boat down on the fish. As usually happens during this operation I got soaked with water continually slopping in over the flat transom but I was totally unaware of being wet. My whole effort was put into line recovery, and it was gratifying to find the previously half-emptied spool of the big reel rapidly starting to fill up again.

The marlin soon woke up to the fact that the hated boat was rapidly bearing down on it, and for the second time the great fish stopped and began to circle. I always believe in working myself and a big fish as hard as I can, and it was not long before I had the marlin in sight. Twice more it tried to run but, by this time, it was too tired to put up much more than a token fight. Finally, the trace swivel was wound out of the water and, as the mate's fist closed over the leader, the fish surfaced to wallow in the wave troughs.

That marlin took me exactly 40 minutes to beat on gear of 80 pound class. At a weight of 561 pounds and a length of a fraction over 12 feet it was big enough to win the contest, giving me the glory of winning a world championship. Had it managed to dive to a depth of 300 or 400 yards the outcome might well have been very different, for not only is a deep diving fish difficult to pump back to the surface there is also the very real and ever present danger of an attack by sharks.

The intense vibrations set up by a hard fighting fish attract shark and help them to home in on a hooked fish. And a hooked fish, irrespective of species, has little chance to evade an attacking shark and, of course, once the fish has been bitten it falls easy prey to its attacker.

Another factor to be considered is that mutilated fish are automatically disqualified under IGFA rules, and many a tournament has been lost through great fish being savaged by sharks.

My good friend Captain Francisco Van Uden, of San Miguel Island, Azores caught a magnificent 500 pound plus blue marlin that took a Kona Head, jumped twice and promptly dived to a depth of nearly 2,000 feet where it expired. As I've mentioned, marlin are inclined to do this. Probably because sudden exertion combined with an abrupt change in pressure causes the fish's heart to fail. When this situation occurs there are only two ways out of the problem.
1. The angler can cut the line and allow the fish to sink forever.
2. He can make up his mind to raise the carcase inch by tortuous inch, using his body and rod as a crude form of crane.

This is exactly what Francisco Van Uden decided to do. After its initial plunge the huge fish never moved by itself again. To Francisco, this fish was more than important: for one thing it was a huge fish, and for another it was the first blue marlin ever taken on rod and line from the Azores archipelago.

Several hours later – and with only half the line back on the reel – Francisco was still lifting that giant fish, an inch at a time. After many more hours of back breaking effort, the great fish was hauled to the surface. Knowing the area to hold many blue and mako shark, Francisco was amazed to find his fish intact with not a mark, not a scratch, to mar its pristine beauty.

Later, back at the dock in Porta Delgada, this first Azores marlin was hoisted up and ceremoniously weighed in. Not all marlin stories end in success. I was once fishing off Madeira when a truly gigantic blue marlin was sighted. Most marlin from the waters off Madeira weigh over 500 pounds, while several have been caught over 900 pounds, and one 1,000-pound specimen has been successfully beaten on rod and line.

The fish we were after looked to be over 700 pounds in weight, which put it well into the big marlin bracket. It was idling on the surface, obviously basking in the hot Madeiran sun. Such fish can usually be approached fairly easily and sometimes they will deign to take a well-presented bait. Five times we trolled a natural deadbait of mullet directly in front of the fish, but not once did it show interest. Then a local commercial boat en route for Funchal Harbour noticed us circling in a given area. As they approached the sharp eyes of their lookout sighted the telltale dorsal fin. Instantly they rigged up a live mackerel and just as instantly the marlin took it. That fish weighed in at over 800 pounds. A triumph for the commercial skipper and a hard lesson learned by us sport fishermen.

WHITE MARLIN

Never a particularly common species, the white marlin is an attractive fish capable of putting on a dazzling show of aerobatics when hooked. White marlin are sometimes found off the Canary Islands, Madeira and the Azores, but it is only the Canary Islands and the Azores which appear, as yet, to produce these fish on a regular basis. By bill-fish standards the white marlin is a diminutive fish. Most rod-caught specimens weighing between 40 and 60 pounds, although fish of twice this weight occasionally occur.

What the white marlin lacks in size it makes up for in fighting spirit. Aggressive in the extreme, a white marlin hooked on appropriate tackle can put up a magnificent fight. Unfortunately, far too many white marlin are hooked on heavy tackle designed for the much larger blue marlin and on this sort of gear the average white marlin does not stand a chance. Selective fishing, using appropriate tackle, is undoubtedly the answer. But in European waters where there is as much chance of hooking a giant blue marlin as there is of catching a smaller white, few anglers will take the risk of using light tackle and then losing the blue marlin of a lifetime as the direct result.

Tackle

Rods

To get the best out of white marlin, a 20 pound or 30 pound IGFA rod should be used. Rods of this weight are perfect for playing out even a hard-fighting, monster white marlin. Many anglers, however, prefer to compromise and use a rod with a 50 pound class rating. This is less sporting for white marlin than the use of a lighter rod but does give the angler a little extra chance should a blue marlin decide to intercept the bait.

Reels and Lines

The perfect reels to use when fishing for white marlin are the 20 pound or 30 pound class Penn International models. These reels can be loaded with nylon or monofilament of the appropriate breaking strain to suit rod and reel capabilities.

Baits and Lures

White marlin are active feeders, often showing a more aggressive approach than blue marlin. A hungry white marlin is quite prepared to tackle lures or baits intended for blue marlin. Personally I prefer to use smaller lures. A combination of natural bait and plastic skirt (see Fig. 11) can often be a

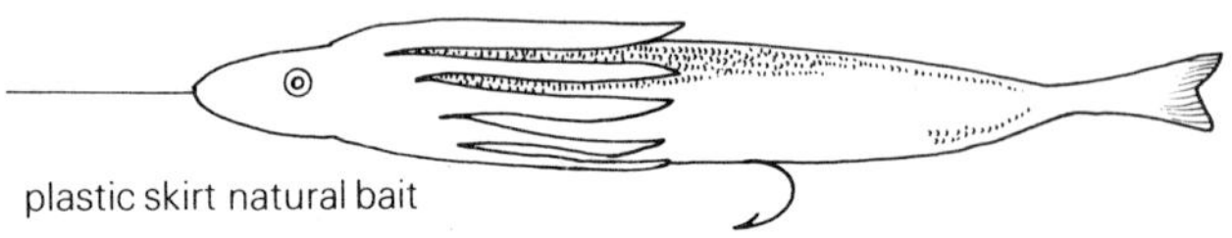

FIGURE 11   A combination bait of natural fish covered at the head with plastic skirt is deadly for white marlin.

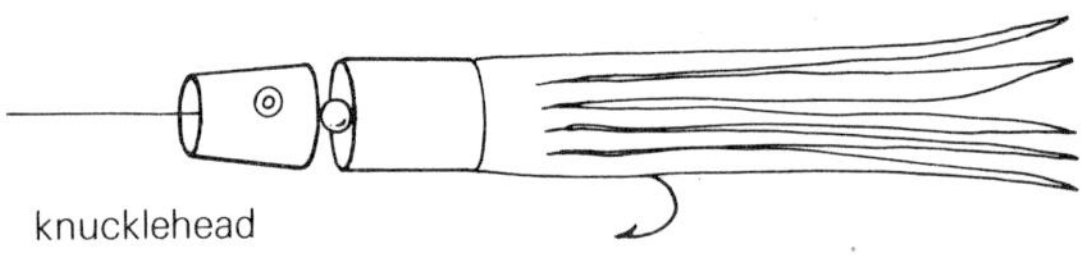

FIGURE 12   Knucklehead lures are also highly effective when fishing for white marlin.

killer where white marlin are concerned. Medium length Kona Heads or knuckleheads (see Fig. 12) are also highly effective. In my experience once attracted to a bait, white marlin are more difficult to alarm than blue marlin.

Due to their comparatively small mouth-size they can be difficult to hook. But once a white marlin has followed – or struck at – a bait without becoming hooked it is worth turning the boat round to fish the same area as white marlin can often be induced to strike again.

Location and Methods

The largest white marlin I have ever caught weighed 120 pounds and fought like a fury. This fish – huge for its species – was caught during a tournament and gave me a very good chance of winning the coveted White Marlin Trophy. Unfortunately for me, another angler caught a white of just 5 pounds heavier and walked away with the trophy. The chance of two such white marlin being taken in one day from one area must be millions to one.

Few marlin anglers normally ever see a fish of a 100 pound plus let alone catch one. Up to about 80 pounds is the norm for a good fish with this species and over 90 pounds in weight any white marlin can be classed as a specimen. Luck has a great

42

deal to do with catching white marlin. In the season of 1983 I tried fishing for white marlin out from the island of San Miguel in the Azores. The same fishing grounds had previously provided hot action with blue marlin and tuna, and several white marlin had been sighted but not hooked.

On this particular day the Azores were basking under their usual ridge of high pressure and, with not the slightest hint of wind, the Atlantic lay in a mirror-like calm. In these sort of conditions bill fish can often be sighed basking on the surface but on this day, however, the only fins in view belonged to big blue shark.

Our intended fishing ground was *Mar De Plata* (silver sea) which lay some 14 miles out from the harbour of Porta Delgada. Lures were put out almost as soon as we cleared the magnificent harbour, for like all the volcanic islands of the Atlantic around San Miguel the land instantly falls into depths of 100 fathoms (600 feet) or more. Marlin seldom come inside a 100 fathom line but in the Azores – with truly deep water situated so close to the land – marlin can be expected at any time.

We were just over halfway to Mar De Plata when I suddenly saw a broad silver flash directly astern of one of my lures. Instinctively I reached for the rod just as the fish snatched at the lure. For a brief second I thought the fish was taken but it had missed the hooks. I knew, however, from my glimpse of the fish that it was a white marlin. I had seen and caught plenty of these in the Bahamas and hoped that this fish would follow the normal pattern of its tribe and return to take the bait a second time. I knew too from the brief but broad flash of the marlin's side that it was a big fish, at least, 'big' as white marlin go.

It is always impossible to put an accurate weight on any fish that is seen only for a split second, but from what I had glimpsed this fish was a real specimen. As the boat circled back to quarter the same area of sea, I kept a careful eye on the two baits. Suddenly the fish was back, materialising out of nowhere to take up a watchful position a yard or so astern of the red and yellow lure. It was slightly nervous, possibly it had been pricked on its first attempt to eat the lure. It was also definitely hungry, and I could only wait and hope that its urgent need to fill its belly would overcome its apparent fear of the bait.

Abruptly, the fish made up its mind. I was close enough to see it turn slightly on its side and, as its bill appeared out of the water, I saw its jaws close on the lure. With the reel locked up on strike drag the fish felt the hook and immediately began to jump.

Once, twice, three times it came up throwing out a shower of spray like a fountain in the clear area around it. As it bounced out for the fourth time I distinctly saw the bait propelled from its jaws. A split second later the fish was gone for ever.

A typical marlin luck. Two chances at one fish, a hook up, and then the bait and hook is thrown free!

Shark Fishing

This has long been popular sport with European big game anglers. At one time the rather sluggish blue shark was the most popular target species and anglers from all over Europe travelled to the Cornish ports of Looe, Mevagissey and, to a lesser extent, Falmouth to catch blue shark.

Looe was such a popular sharking venue that the Shark Club of Great Britain was established in this port. The club still flourishes and has done much in its time to pioneer the sport of shark fishing. Many porbeagle and mako were also caught from Looe but it was not until the now famous Isle of Wight shark grounds were located that European shark fishing took its giant stride forward.

The Isle of Wight grounds produced many huge porbeagle and thresher shark and proved that big shark could be taken in reasonable numbers in British waters. Later still, the porbeagle hunters moved their activities to the coast of North Devon while the serious thresher-shark anglers continued (and continue) to fish the St Catherine's Point area of the Isle of Wight, usually with spectacular results.

As European anglers learned about shark fishing many expert anglers turned their attention to the coast and islands of Portugal. It was soon established that venues like Madeira, the Azores and the Canary Islands could produce not only blue and mako shark but also the more exotic species as well: hammerhead, white tip, six gill and even white shark could be caught from their waters. This increased the general interest in shark fishing, which in turn produced some fine catches of very large shark.

Shark fishing is a justifiably popular sport. Almost any angler can afford a place on a shark boat, and for this reason shark are often unfairly referred to as the poor man's big game fish. Interest in shark fishing continues to grow annually and with luck this trend will continue, for shark fishing is a rough, tough sport worth a little of any angler's time and money.

Tackle

Rods

It is customary for most charter boats going after shark to carry a selection of made-up rods which prospective anglers can hire by the day. Unfortunately for the customers most of this hire tackle is far too heavy to give the average run of shark even the slightest sporting chance.

Serious shark anglers, however, prefer to use their own lighter equipment. Most rod makers now produce a range of hollow glass rods suitable for shark fishing. Most of these rods comply with IGFA standards, with the 50 and 80 pound class rods being ideal for all aspects of shark fishing.

For blue shark the 50 pound class rod is ideal, while for porbeagle, mako and thresher the 80 pound class rod should be used. When purchasing a rod specifically for shark fishing, it is always advisable to pay particular attention to the rod fittings and rings. Most manufacturers produce high quality rods, but there are still some rogue rod makers on the loose who sell reasonable rods fitted with inferior fittings.

When using a shark rod I like one fitted with full roller rings: the best rings being the American-made AFTCO type. These have been copied in the Far East but the copies are *never* up to the quality of the originals. So insist on AFTCO and you will not go far wrong. Reel fittings too should be of the highest quality you can afford.

Always remember that a shark rod may well have to subdue a record fish. Failing this, it will undoubtedly be used to catch many very large fish, so once again it pays to invest in the best rod you can afford. In general, as with most things, the more you spend the better the quality of the rod and its furnishings.

Reels

Your choice of reel for shark fishing will depend entirely on individual taste. The majority of experienced shark anglers prefer large-capacity multiplier reels of the Penn Senator or Tatler type.

Penn also produce a series of Tournament reels, fitted with a lever drag system rather than with the star drag type. Personally, I do not think that lever drag reels are suitable or should be used for shark fishing. The old fashioned star drag reels still function perfectly, and cost far less than the Tournament reels. For heavy shark work a Tatler V or a Penn Senator 9-0 is ideal. Both reels have similar line capacity, although the lighter British-made Tatler reel is – in my opinion – the better of the two types.

The current cost of a good-quality shark reel ranges from £50/$70 upwards, depending upon the size and make of reel you require. Although good second-hand, shark-sized reels can often be obtained for a lot less than this. In Britain the 'Swap Shop' page of *Anglers Mail* is often full of suitable reels being offered at bargain prices, and most other countries have similar pages in their angling papers and magazines. I have purchased several shark reels through 'Swap Shop', and every one has been a bargain.

Lines

Most shark are caught on float-fished baits. Because of this it is best to use a line which has a natural buoyancy; ordinary nylon lines being of little use for shark fishing. Probably the best line to use is dacron which I have talked about in earlier chapters. It is made of braided polyester fibres, and is imported from America. This makes it expensive, but being rot proof the line lasts for many seasons and so is worth the money.

A cheaper, good quality line is the British-made Sea Ranger brand, manufactured from braided terylene. The beauty of braided line is that it floats and will not stretch. Lack of

47

elasticity is important when hunting big game fish, for it is very difficult to keep in contact with a big fish if the line continually stretches when pressure is applied to it.

The actual breaking strain of the line you use will depend entirely on the type and size of shark you expect to encounter. If, for example, a blue shark is your main quarry you could confidently fish with a line of a 50 pound breaking strain. If, on the other hand, porbeagles or threshers are known to exist in the area you intend to fish, then you would be far safer using a heavier line.

Unfortunately for the sport, many anglers and boatmen take things to extremes and purchase lines which are far too heavy for the job in hand. Lines of 120 pound breaking strain are commonly used on blue shark of a third of that weight, with the result that anything other than a truly enormous fish can easily be hauled in to the gaff within minutes of setting the hook. The argument used against lighter lines is, of course, the possibility of hooking a real monster of one type or another. But if this does happen, then the angler simply has to take things easy. Instead of bullying the fish into submission, the angler will have to settle down to a long and careful battle – which, after all, is the sporting part of shark fishing.

Where I do most of my British-waters' shark fishing, porbeagles of well over 400 pounds in weight are known to exist and the average fish weigh from 150 pounds upwards. Because of this high average size I habitually use a line with an 80 pound breaking strain. Other anglers use heavier lines still and, even so, from time to time we all get broken up by fish which we just cannot handle. But for normal everyday sharking I find that the 80 pound line will do all I ask of it and still give the average shark a little leeway to show off its fighting spirit.

All dacron lines have an IGFA rating or breaking point. Officially this is 10 percent below the stated breaking strain of the line: thus the 80 pound dacron should break at a 72 pound pull. Sea Ranger lines, on the other hand, break well above their stated breaking strain. I point this out for the record conscious anglers. Break a record on anything other than IGFA-approved line and your chances of making the record books become slimmer. A point to remember when you next purchase some line.

Hooks

For general shark fishing in Britain a selection of hooks ranging in size from 10-0 to size 16-0 should be carried. Mustads make the strongest hooks, and most up-to-date tackle shops keep a good supply of shark-size hooks in stock. Choice of hook size depends on two things – the size of the bait being used, and the size of the shark expected to take it.

Small blue shark, for example, can be caught on smallish mackerel or pilchard baits, so there is seldom a necessity to use a hook size larger than 10-0. For big porbeagle, thresher or mako, however, the required bait consisting of two large mackerel or a 4-pound pollack or mullet would mask the point of a small hook, so a 12, a 14 or 16-0 should be used.

Finally, a word of warning. Fish hooks of all sizes – but particularly very large ones – are normally blunt when bought. Each hook should be carefully sharpened with a carborundum stone, both before and during use. This is vitally important, as a large blunt hook is impossible to set in the hard mouth of a shark.

The best shark hook I have ever used is the Mustad Seamaster, which has an offset point. Such hooks are easy to set on the strike. Flat forged hooks are to be avoided. I bought and used some American Pfleuger shark hooks, all of which have at some point pulled out of hooked fish. My personal advice is to stick to Mustad Seamasters, that way you may manage to avoid this problem.

Traces

Shark traces should always be made of wire. The sharp teeth of even a small shark will quickly cut through soft trace materials. Moreover, the rough hide of a shark will chafe through anything other than wire.

Shark traces can be bought ready-made from tackle shops or else made up at home. I have all my shark traces made up by a local, yacht rigging-wire specialist, who makes them using galvanised multi-strand wire. Each trace is made up in two equal 8 foot lengths joined in the centre by a 5-0 heavy duty swivel. On one end I have the hook, on the other a second 5-0 swivel. Each trace can be used a number of times.

Any shark fishing trace must be at least 16 foot long, for it should have enough length – at all times – to keep the actual fishing line clear of the shark's rough skin. The addition of swivels helps to eliminate the problem of a trace kinking and therefore being weakened during the time it takes for a good fish to be played out. A less expensive, but highly effective shark trace can be made from suitable lengths of Bowden (or similar) bicycle brake cable. This kind of wire is strong, supple and easy to obtain. To make a join, the wire should be passed through the hook or swivel, doubled back and the two strands lashed together with a short length of thin, soft, case wire. The whole join should then be soldered over, after which it should hold any shark that swims! This very useful tip was passed on to me by a well-known British angler, Bob Bradshaw from Bournemouth, Dorset.

Never use a trace which has become kinked or shows rust spots, it is not worth losing your catch. A big shark can easily snap a faulty trace so check your trace carefully both before and after using it. If the trace shows a defect, then scrap it. It *could* cost you a record breaker.

Shark Floats

Although it is possible to purchase ready-made floats that are large enough for shark fishing, the majority of experienced shark anglers much prefer to manufacture their own, from any buoyant material that comes easily to hand. Empty plastic detergent or photographic-developer bottles are the firm favourites. These need little adaptation to turn them into very serviceable floats which besides being cheap and easy to make have the added advantage of being virtually unbreakable.

The simplest way to turn one of these containers into a sliding float is to tie a short length of old line tightly round the neck of the bottle, then attach a single swivel to the loose end of the line (see Fig. 13). The reel line can then be threaded through the open eye of the swivel and attached to the trace.

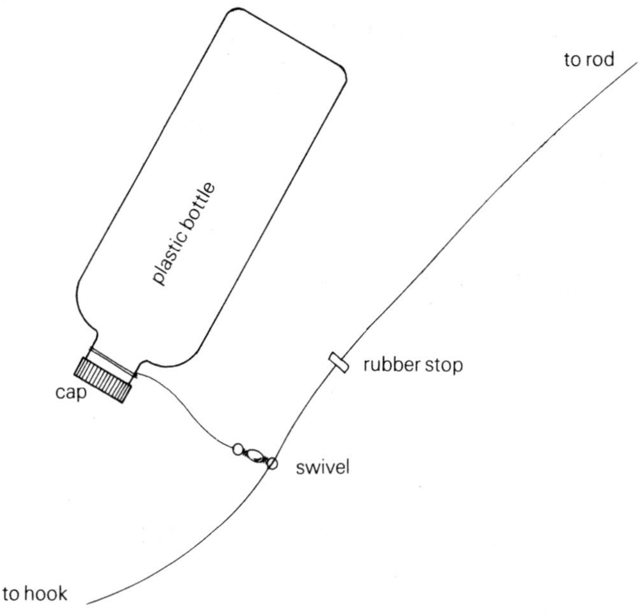

FIGURE 13   A cheap and easy to make shark float constructed from an empty plastic bottle, a short length of old line, a rubber stop and a swivel.

The newly-made bottle float is now free to slide up the line. Before use a rubber stop can be added at whatever distance one intends to fish, and the tackle is set to go.

Balloons also make very good shark floats. These can either be tied directly to the reel line or else attached by means of a swivel. The shape of the balloon is immaterial, but it is essential not to over inflate it otherwise a taking shark may well feel the drag of the too bouyant balloon and drop the bait. The trouble with using balloon floats is that cruising sharks are often attracted to the colour of the balloon. This is particularly true of the porbeagle, and on several occasions I have had a porbeagle shark bite the balloon, severing the reel line in the process.

Gaffs

Every charter boat engaged in shark fishing carries a selection of large shark gaffs. The individual boat owner who hopes to try his luck with the occasional shark fishing trip is well advised to follow suit. Three very big gaffs are essential, and all should be attached to the boat by a 4 fathom (24 foot) rope, so that if a gaffed fish does tear the gaff out of someone's hands the gaff will still be tied to the boat and can be hauled in without undue trouble.

The ideal shark gaff is the breaking type, where the head and handle part on impact. This type of gaff is made in Britain by Grice & Young of Christchurch, Dorset.

Sundry Items

A butt socket and shoulder harness are advisable for catching big shark, as they alleviate much of the strain and discomfort of trying to play a really big fish on a plain rod.

Bare trace wire can lacerate your hands very badly, so when grasping a long trace before gaffing a shark always wear a pair of leather gauntlets. My own are of the industrial type, which completely protect my fingers from injury.

A large and lively shark can be very difficult and dangerous to handle once it has been brought inboard. Because of this most professional skippers carry a 'priest' in the shape of a hammer, mallet or length of lead pipe. A couple of heavy blows on the tip of the shark's snout will often kill the fish immediately.

Hooking a Shark Bait

All experienced shark anglers have their own way of hooking and presenting a bait. Some carefully remove a portion of the backbone, then thread the hook through the bait in such a way that the hook point and barb project from the back of the fish. Some pass the hook through the tail and round the body of the bait, ending up with the hook through the gills and out of the mouth (see Fig. 14). Others use a simpler method – the one I prefer – which is to pass the hook right through the tail section of the bait so that it hangs head down from the bend of the hook. To make sure the bait stays firmly in place, the wrist of the bait's tail is often lashed to the shank of the hook (see Fig. 15). Two whole fish can be mounted as bait one above the

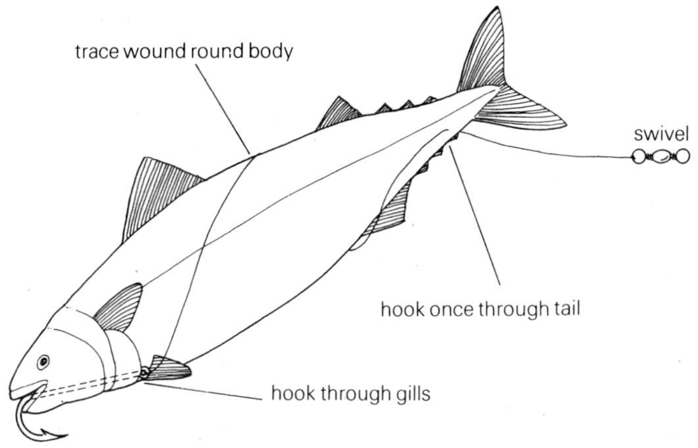

FIGURE 14   One way of hooking a shark bait is to pass the hook through the tail section, wrap the trace round the body of the bait and pass the hook through the gills so that the point and bend project from the bait's mouth.

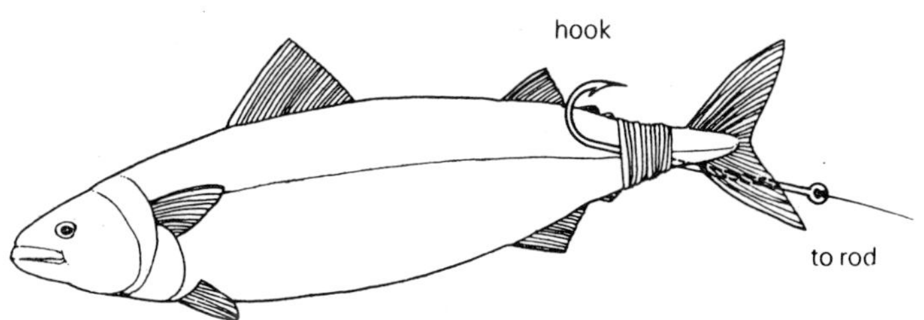

FIGURE 15   Another simpler way of hooking a shark bait is to pass the hook through the tail section of the bait, then lash the wrist of the tail to the hook with wire, wool or elastic.

other. Alternatively, the bait or baits can be hooked just once, through the eye sockets and left hanging from the bend of the hook.

This last method leaves the actual flesh of the bait totally unbroken – an advantage in rough water, which quickly breaks up a bait hooked through the body. The bony eye sockets do not tear easily and a bait hooked in this way will stay on the hook for an indefinite period.

Location and Methods

The most important single factor in successful shark fishing is the 'rubby dubby' trail. You can have the best rod, reel, line and bait in the world but without adequate dubby your chance of success is virtually nil. By 'adequate' I mean both in quality and quantity.

To lay a successful, long and thick rubby dubby trail calls for a minimum of twenty stone (125 kilograms) of finely minced fish (mackerel and horse mackerel are excellent) mixed with pure pilchard oil and bran. This is trailed behind the boat in a perforated container. To add to this trail, chunks of cut fish should also be thrown out of the boat, to lay a thin but steady line of titbits that will encourage scavenging sharks to feed.

Once the shark grounds are reached the angler's first job is to hang the rubby dubby container over the side or stern of the boat. In the British West Country most sharkers use a wickerwork fish basket as a rubby dubby container, but a large mesh bag can also be used.

Very few fishermen anchor a boat while shark fishing and normally the technique used is to drift broadside on with the tide. As the boat wallows along, the movement of water against the rubby dubby container will keep a continual flow of fish oil and flesh particles washing away from the boat. This slick will trail out for several miles and any shark that comes across the trail will follow it up to within a catchable distance of the boat. To keep a good slick going all the time it is necessary to pay strict attention to the container, adding fresh quantities of mashed-up fish at frequent intervals.

Once a satisfactory bait trail can be seen streaming away from the boat, the shark tackle should be baited and put over the side. Under no circumstances should more than three or, at the very most, four rods be used at any one time. Otherwise a hooked fish may collect other lines as it runs out and the resulting tangle can take hours to sort out. Worse still, two or even three shark might be hooked simultaneously. I have seen this happen several times and on each occasion all the fish were lost in the resulting chaos.

Shark are liable to feed at almost any depth. To find out just how deep they are on any given day it is advisable to set each bait at different depths. For example, a boat fishing three rods should set the distance between float and bait at 20, 40 and 60 feet respectively. The rig which catches the first fish will automatically reveal the most-likely taking depth for that particular day and the other tackles can be changed to correspond in depth with the successful one.

Most shark, other than thresher tend to swim and feed fairly near the surface. And on hot calm days, particularly during periods of fine settled weather, they tend to stay near the surface at all times, and so in these conditions the tackle can be set accordingly at, say 15, 25 and 35 feet. However, when the weather is rough and the water colder it is those baits fished well-down towards the sea bed that are most likely to produce shark.

Although, as yet, no one knows much about the movement and feeding habits of thresher shark, it is fairly certain that under normal circumstances they are a bottom feeding species.

In view of this it would probably be better when after thresher to choose a likely mark and anchor on it, rather than fish on the drift in conventional shark fishing style. Most of the threshers I have seen caught were taken in this way on normal shark weight gear but with a running ledger as opposed to the standard float fishing rig used for other types of shark. Large threshers have, of course, been taken from time to time on float tackle but never in quantity.

Whenever a shark bait is in the water, the drag of the reel should be off, so that a fish which takes the bait can run with the line without any check to its movements. Far too many anglers are content to leave a shark rod to fish for itself. This is wrong. Although it is not necessary or practical to sit holding the rod at all times, the float should be kept under constant observation, so that the moment a fish takes the bait loose line can be pulled off the reel, giving the fish a chance to take the bait decisively. For shark, contrary to popular belief, do not simply rush up and swallow the bait in savage fashion: very often, quite the reverse applies. And I have had strikes from large porbeagles which have hardly caused the float to move at all.

As with most fish, shark bites normally follow a definite pattern. First the float will bob down several times, as the fish mouths at the bait. If it is satisfied that there is no danger, the fish will then move off, usually fairly slowly, gathering speed as it goes. This is the critical time for at the first sign of drag the fish will open its mouth and eject the bait. However, provided that the angler has seen the preliminary movements and is holding the rod and feeding out loose line as the shark moves off, the shark can usually be relied upon to swallow the bait with confidence.

Judging the exact moment to strike takes experience, but it is worth remembering that shark will often slow up as they begin to swallow bait. If they do not, then it will be necessary to strike as the fish is running off at speed. More shark are lost on the strike than at any other time. The fight of a hooked shark varies considerably. Some will give up without the slightest struggle: others will fight long, hard and furiously.

When drifting for shark, the boatman must always be prepared to start his engine and follow a hooked fish. This is particularly true of large mako or porbeagle which will, if left to their own devices, soon run out every inch of line on the reel. Even so, it does not pay to keep the boat too close in to a well-hooked fish: for the drag imposed by a hundred yards or more of heavy braided line will help to wear out even a very big fish in a fairly short period of time.

Most shark when hooked try to put as much distance between themselves and the boat as possible. This however is not always the case and some never make a run. I once hooked a brute of a shark – in British waters, on the Isle of Wight grounds – which simply hung around the boat and totally ignored the constant pressure of the heavy tackle I was using. Even while I played the first fish a second shark, estimated at over 200 pounds, was nuzzling at the rubby dubby container right under my rod tip.

I have never hooked another shark as powerful as this one anywhere else round the waters of the British Isles and can only presume it to have been a really huge specimen. I finally lost it when it passed under the boat and fouled my reel line on the keel of the fishing boat.

A big shark should always be tied up, tail first, to the boat then clubbed, not brought aboard.

There is evidence to show that it is sometimes possible to catch shark out of the normally recognised season. Despite the widely-held belief that all shark migrate to warmer climes with the onset of winter, commercial fishermen around the coasts of Cornwall often encounter big shark while winter fishing for mackerel, herring or pilchard. Winter shark fishing may, then, be a distinct possibility. Only time and effort can show whether or not these fish remain behind in sufficient numbers to make them a worthwhile proposition for the winter boat angler.

Blue Shark

The blue shark is a streamlined fish which gets its name from a distinctive dark blue back and light blue sides. Unfortunately these beautiful colours fade to a drab grey once the fish has been killed. Blue shark weighing over 200 pounds have been caught in British waters off Cornwall and there is evidence to show that these fish can exceed a weight of over 300 pounds.

In warmer climates blue shark can grow to a huge size. I once caught a 448 pound blue shark off the Azores. Unfortunately for me I did not realise at the time that my fish broke the existing world record by 38 pounds. And in consequence the record for this species still stands at 410.

I doubt whether fish of much over 300 pounds will ever occur off the coast of Britain. The average size of rod-caught blue shark is probably less than 60 pounds and many fish in the 40 pound class are caught and destroyed each season. The minimum qualifying weight for membership of the Shark Club of Great Britain is 75 pounds, and any fish topping a hundred can justifiably be regarded as a good catch.

Catches of up to thirty blue shark have been made in a single day off Cornwall, but few experienced shark fishermen really regard the average blue shark as a sporting proposition. On standard shark-fishing tackle the majority put up little or no fight and can be played out and gaffed in a remarkably short space of time. The vast bulk of shark caught in the West

Country fall to novice holiday-makers who, while enjoying themselves, in all probability have never fished before or since. Naturally enough, these people are apt to prolong the fight as they struggle with unfamiliar tackle and thrill to the pull of a large fish which, to them, is a dangerous man-eater of uncertain temperament. The knowledgeable angler, however, usually goes blue sharking with a set of fairly light tackle in an attempt to get some reasonable sport from any fish that is hooked.

Blue shark make an ideal starting species for the novice shark angler. And two seasons of blue sharking are enough to develop the necessary skills needed to fish for the more hard-hitting porbeagle, mako and thresher shark.

Porbeagle Shark

The first big catches of porbeagle shark from British waters were made off the Isle of Wight. Even now, a decade or more later, we still know very little really about these fish; although it is certain that 'beagles' weighing at least 500 pounds live and hunt in the seas off the British coast. It is also possible that much larger fish live as yet undetected in Britain's seas.

In August 1971, two friends and I hooked and boated twelve shark in a single day while boat fishing five miles south east of St Catherine's Point in Isle of Wight waters. The smallest shark taken weighed exactly 120 pounds and I was fortunate enough to hook a huge porbeagle, which we estimated at 450 pound plus. I was also unfortunate enough to lose the same fish twenty minutes later when it dived under the drifting boat and snagged and smashed my line of 80 pound breaking strain braided terylene.

Unlike blue shark, which tend to swim and feed well away from land, porbeagles have a tendency to cruise close to the shore in search of food. One well-known Irish angler, Jack Shie, distinguished himself by actually catching a number of big porbeagles from the shore. All of these fish were taken by float fishing, using a beach casting rod and 18 or 20 pound breaking strain line; truly a remarkable piece of fishing.

The boat angler wishing to try his luck with shark would be well advised to keep fairly close to the coastline at all times. I have seen big porbeagles basking in less than 40 foot of water, and some of Britain's most productive grounds off North Devon are not much deeper than this, proving conclusively that deep water is by no means the porbeagle's natural habitat. And I have noticed, many times, that this particular species of shark is attracted by strong tides and by overspill areas. The dangerous tide race off St Catherine's Point and Hartland Point is a good example of this and is probably the main reason why big shark congregate in that area.

As a sporting species, the porbeagle has much to offer a big game angler. A beautiful fish, its thick muscular body and long fins give it a powerful appearance. Any angler lucky enough to make contact with a specimen weighing upwards of a hundred pounds will very soon realise just how much strength and endurance a big porbeagle can muster. There is absolutely no comparison between this fish and the far less exciting blue shark, for a porbeagle in good condition is a true game fish capable of providing even an expert angler with some truly thrilling fishing.

One of the greatest battles I've had with a big fish came when I hooked and boated a shark which may or may not have been a porbeagle. This fish was taken off the Isle of Wight and was my fifth fish of the day. Its speed was incredible. Far faster than any other porbeagle I have ever hooked. At one time we had to run the boat's engines flat out to keep up with it. Oddly enough, it was not even a big fish. When weighed it tipped the scales at just 168 pounds.

In appearance it resembled a slimmed-down porbeagle but there the similarity ended. A true porbeagle is grey-brown in colour: this fish was burnished silver. To add to the confusion the skin was covered in tiny dark spots and blotches. In an attempt to solve the mystery, I submitted photographs of the fish to the Natural History Museum in London for identification. Unfortunately, I did not submit the body and without it complete identification was impossible. The Natural History Museum did, however, state that this fish may possibly have been a shark of an unknown species. Since this catch I have heard reports of two more spotted shark, and been shown photographs of one of them.

In retrospect, I feel that these fish were in all probability, porbeagles with unusual pigmentation. Until another such fish is caught and turned over to the Museum I will never know for certain whether I am right or wrong in my guess about the identity of my fish.

Thresher Shark

The thresher shark is a very distinctive fish. The upper lobe of its tail is almost as long as its body, giving it a rakish overall appearance.

Thresher are far more common in European waters than is generally supposed, although they are seldom hooked by the sport fisherman. No one can say for certain just how prolific this species is, for by nature the thresher is almost exclusively a bottom feeder and only occasionally appears on the surface. Its name derives from the shark's habit of using its great scythe-like tail to thresh the water in an attempt to round up small shoals of fish. I have actually seen a number of individual thresher shark rounding up shoal mackerel in this way: a truly spectacular sight. Hundreds of mackerel were in the air at one time, all trying to avoid the thrashing tails of several sharks. There is much evidence to show that groups of thresher work together in unison to take full advantage of shoaling fish.

From the rod-and-line point of view, the thresher is a game and gallant opponent. I base my opinion on personal experience, having caught several of these fish myself as well as being present when other specimens have been hooked. The main reason why so few thresher shark are caught by anglers is that no one actually goes out deliberately to fish for them. The odd ones that are hooked usually fall to conventional off-the-bottom shark fishing techniques. I am certain, however, that true bottom fishing is the only really practical way to catch these fish on a regular basis.

In my opinion, the finest thresher shark marks in British waters are off the Isle of Wight. Several seasons ago I wrote an article on this in *Anglers Mail,* and within weeks the grounds off the Isle of Wight had produced a new record for the species. August is undoubtedly the prime month for fishing thresher shark off the Island. Very heavy female threshers arrive in the area during this month to give birth. I have seen thresher shark that exceeded 500 pounds during this period and I am sure that fish of over 600 pounds weight are a possibility from this area.

I often hear reports of tope anglers hooking immense and totally unstoppable fish, said to be monster tope. In all probability these are medium-sized threshers. Thresher shark to just under 300 pounds have been caught on rod and line but it seems likely that, in European waters, these shark can reach a weight of at least 800 pounds.

Mako Shark

The mako is the aristocrat of the shark tribe, a handsome streamlined nomadic fish, which is highly sought after the world over by most true game fishermen.

Mako shark have been caught for many years in the English Channel and mistakenly identified as porbeagle. In 1956, however, the teeth from a supposed record porbeagle were sent to the headquarters of the International Game Fish Association in America where they were positively identified as mako teeth.

An Atlantic fish that occasionally ventures into the mouth of the English Channel, the mako may well reach weights of over 700 pounds. I can find no record of mako further east than Start Point in Devon, and it seems unlikely that many fish venture much further up-Channel than Rame Head.

Falmouth in Cornwall is probably the best place in Britain to visit if you wish to catch a mako shark. Frank and Robin Vinicome of Falmouth currently being the two most experienced mako skippers in the British Isles. Frank Vinicome told me of a possible 1,000 pound mako that one of his anglers fought for many hours before finally losing the fish. And Frank believes that another fish of a thousand pounds is a possibility, even now when mako shark seem to have become a declining species.

I would doubt very much whether any mako shark yet caught in this country was taken deliberately by an angler after mako, for all those I have seen caught, or heard about, have fallen to blue shark baits and tackle.

I once hooked myself a good mako while drifting several miles out beyond the Eddystone Lighthouse. This fish, like most mako shark, went away with a rush and jumped clean out of the water as I set the hook. Although not a monster it did weigh over 200 pounds and, true to type, made me fight hard and long for every inch of line I gained. Only one-in-five or so hooked mako attempt to jump. But when a mako does go up it is an unforgettable sight. No fish in the world – marlin included – jumps as high or as spectacularly as a fighting mako.

I have hooked fish that have certainly cleared the water by 20 feet. The best was several years ago when – while fishing in the Azores – I had a terrific battle with a 540 pounder that put on a really spectacular display of aerobatics. Fortunately enough, I had a Portuguese television crew on the boat and each jump was filmed so that later we were able to watch the film and confirm the height of each of the leaps that this great fish had made.

Not all shark trips end in success and this is the story of one that didn't. I was based in the Azores, operating from the lovely town of Horta on Fayal Island. I had been on the island since May, and by mid-September the winds were beginning to strengthen and I knew it would soon be time to head back to England to forget the Azores and its magnificent fishing until the following year.

This, then, was my last day on the island and it did not look promising. At seven in the morning the sea was choppy, showing long lines of whitecaps outside Horta harbour. Checking the weather forecast, which showed that the wind was not expected to rise, we decided to chance our luck and head for a known shark mark beyond a giant rock stack known as *Castelo Branco* (white castle).

I had caught mako to 540 pounds from this area on previous trips and now I hoped for an even larger specimen. Bait, however, was our immediate problem. Within minutes of clearing the harbour arm I ran out handlines equipped with deep diving paravanes, astern of which silver lures flashed attractively. Paravane rigs are perfect for bait catching, they hold the silver spoon lures down until a fish hits the bait then they automatically turn over and rise to the surface bringing the kicking fish with them. It may not be a sporting method but it's a good way of taking fresh bait, and one which I employ a great deal.

On this day, bait was scarce as the rising wind had obviously put the fish down. Fortunately, however, we found a few large mackerel and with these inboard we headed up to the bay beyond the white castle rocks. Clearing the massive headland, we went on to a distance of approximately three miles off the coast. Here the tide flow was strong and, as the skipper cut the engines, the boat began to drift with the prevailing tide flow. Conditions were far from comfortable and, with only a limited supply of bait, I chose to fish just one rod.

The boat was old. Originally built for the dictator Salazar, she was built as a motor yacht rather than a sport fishing boat and she was not equipped with a fighting chair. Nowadays, of course, the Pescatur Company has excellent big game boats in daily use, but in the early days of Azores' sport fishing the ex-president's boat was the only one available.

The skipper, in those days, was an American who knew a great deal about yachting but little to nothing about sport fishing. Fortunately he was game for anything, which was just as well, for when a shark did appear it was far beyond the average run of fish.

We had drifted for a little over two hours and the sea was choppy enough to make things uncomfortable inside the boat, although I was hoping that the rise and fall of the craft would add movement and life to the bait.

When the strike came, it was a typical mako take: one second nothing, the next a screaming reel, followed by a huge splash as a vast fish barrelled out of the waves in standard mako style. Obviously well hooked the fish looked huge but how huge I was only to find out later.

Mako are invariably good fighters, and this one really put on a show but finally it wore down, and both the skipper and I strained for our first good look at the great fish. For a while it circled deep behind the boat but, eventually, I was able to retrieve all the line and, as the big trace swivel clicked heavily against the rod's tip ring, we got our first real look at the shark. I have caught a great many large mako, but never one as long and as broad as this fish. Its head was huge and its tail enormous.

It looked totally exhausted, moving sluggishly to maintain its position in the tide flow, which was good for with only the skipper and me to handle the fish we knew that we had no chance of dragging it inboard: instead we would have to tie it up alongside, for the long steam back to Horta.

The plan was simple. The skipper would plant his big gaff between its mighty pectoral fins and hang on while I dropped a pair of wire nooses over its mighty tail. We anticipated trouble, but did not get any and the fish was quickly and easily gaffed and tail roped to the side of the boat.

To make absolutely certain, the tail wires were tied securely to a large cleat on the broad gunnel and the trace wire was then wrapped tightly round a handrail. Throughout all this the shark did not move. Looking down on it, we realised from its length and girth that its weight would be over 800 pounds. A European record for a certainty, and possibly even a world record, for it was over 13 feet from tail to nose.

Naturally we were delighted. Despite the poor sea conditions and with only two of us aboard, we had successfully played out and tied down one of the largest mako sharks ever caught on rod and line: all this without the benefit of a fighting chair. At this point I began to feel the pain in my back and arms, and the skipper sensing both my tiredness and elation suggested a glass of brandy before we set off for Horta.

With a full glass each we had just started to toast our spectacular success when the great fish came alive again, in a most dramatic fashion. With one shake of its huge body it snapped the heavy wire trace, and then smashed both of the heavy-cable tail wires. I was not worried even at this stage, for the big gaff was still planted solidly between the fish's broad pectoral fins. However, with its head and tail free it began to lash from side to side, forcing me to let it surge on the heavy gaff rope. Once its tail worked it clear of the boat, it was able to pile on pressure and I decided to refasten the long gaff rope to

The author fighting an Azorian blue marlin *(top)*.

The 'bird-like' mouth of the blue marlin is hard, and losses 'on the take' are common *(above)*.

AZORES
BLUE
MARLIN
OCT. 10TH 1984
WEIGTH = 320 kg
ANGLER
T. JENSEN

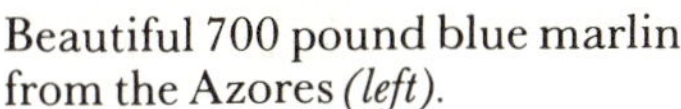

Beautiful 700 pound blue marlin from the Azores *(left)*.

San Miguel in the Azores is fast becoming a marlin 'hot spot' *(top)*.

Bonito make an ideal bait fish for blue marlin. They also provide fine sport on light tackle *(right)*.

Author playing a large blue shark off the Azores *(above)*.

A gaffed blue shark *(top)*.

Large blue shark being boated *(above)*.

Two large blue shark caught by the author, Fayal, Azores *(right)*.

Good porbeagle taken off St Catherine's Point, Isle of Wight in the English Channel *(left)*.

Thresher shark make fine targets for game fishermen *(above)*.

Author with medium weight mako shark *(right)*.

GALHA-A-RÉ
PONTA
DELGADA

Two medium mako, Fayal, Azores *(left)*.

Jaws of a 540 pound mako *(above)*.

Author with 400 pound mako caught in the Azores *(above right)*.

White tip shark being brought to the gaff off Fayal, Azores *(right)*.

Well gaffed white tip *(inset)*.

Author with his second world-record white tip from the Azores *(left)*.

Author with first-ever white tip caught in European waters. It set a new world record *(above)*.

Despite its odd shape a hammerhead fights well when hooked *(above right)*.

Author shows off the jaws of a white tip *(right)*.

Author hooked up on a 192 pound skate in Orkney waters *(above left)*.

Coalfish cut and trimmed for skate bait *(left)*.

Large skate being boated *(top)*. Author's largest skate to date, weight 192 pounds caught off Orkney *(above)*.

Trolling for tuna off Pont San Lurencõ Lighthouse, Madeira *(above)*.

Atlantic big eye tuna caught in Madeiran waters *(left)*.

Yellow fin tuna caught off San Miguel, Azores *(right)*.

Giant blue fin tuna from the
Azores *(left)*.

Skipper Anton Proctor gaffs a fine
ling off the Isle of Wight *(above)*.

Big cod taken from a wreck off the
Isle of Wight *(right)*.

Fine ling from a mid-Channel wreck *(left)*.

Good cod and ling. These fish are typical of those taken by wreck anglers *(above)*.

2,000 + pounds of cod and ling taken from a wreck off the Hampshire coast *(right)*.

Gaffing a good barracuda, Madeira *(left)*.

Fine barracuda on yellow Japanese feathers *(top)*.

Typical European barracuda of average size *(above)*.

Grouper of this size are common off the Atlantic Islands (*top left*).

A dorado, one of the most colourful fish encountered by the European big game angler (*far left*).

Author with 60 pound wahoo. One of the newly discovered game fish of the Atlantic Islands (*left*).

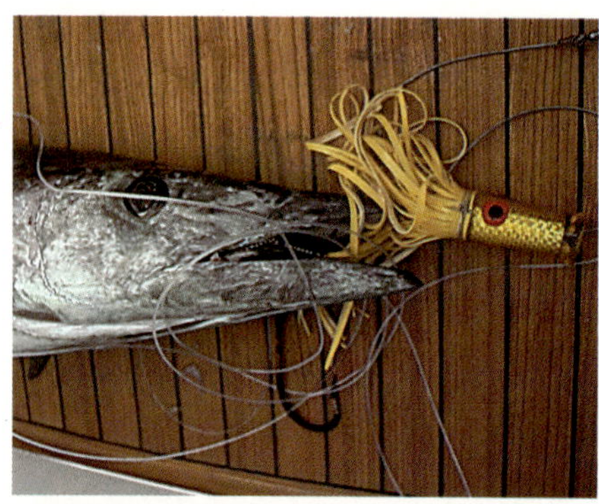

Wahoo with yellow Kona Head lure *(left)*.

Trolling at last light *(below)*.

A large moray caught in the Azores. Eels of this size should be handled with care *(previous page)*.

the double cleat and let the fish wear itself down.

The problem was that the shark had other ideas. It gathered momentum, pulled the heavy rope taut and ripped the cleat right out of the woodwork! Now free of the boat – but still dragging tail rope, gaff and trailing brass cleat – it shot off at speed, turned and struck the side of the boat a tremendous blow with its vast snout.

It hammered into us four times in all, knocking a great splintered hole in the side of the boat, just above the waterline. Having worn off its temper it turned and vanished, probably to die far down in the Atlantic depths. With water pouring in, we did not have time to speculate on its possible fate: we were both far too busy stuffing mattresses into the jagged hole left by the shark.

By pumping out water solidly all the way back we made harbour safely, but that boat had to be lifted out for immediate repairs and what the head of the Tourist Office said when he saw the damage is unprintable. Fortunately, the old boat was repaired ready for my visit the next year, but I never see the president's boat without remembering that great shark. I only hope that it did live, for by now it would be way over world record size. Maybe one day our paths will cross again and if they do, then I hope my luck holds and the shark's does not!

White Tip Shark

Until September 1980 no big game angler had ever encountered a white tip shark in European waters. Then, in the space of one week's fishing off Fayal Island in the Azores, I hooked eight individual white tips, five of which were successfully boated. Prior to this, the only recorded European white tip shark was a single specimen caught in 1954 by a commercial fishing boat operating off Madeira.

When I caught my first European specimen I was already familiar with the species. I had seen several caught while fishing off Yucatan in Mexico, but none of these were of the size of the fish I sighted and caught off the Azores.

On that day in 1980 when I caught my first Azores white tip

we were fishing over the peak of an underwater mountain some fourteen miles off Fayal Island. This area is well known for its rich bottom fishing and is called the Baixa Do Condor (condor bank). At its shallowest point, the bank is 120 fathoms (720 feet) deep: while on its outside edge depths of over 500 fathoms (3,000 feet) have been recorded.

At all times of the year the Condor Bank is a hot-spot for shark of many kinds, drawn, no doubt, by the abundance of food fish on the bottom. Large blue shark are common there, and on more than one occasion I have caught a brace of fine mako shark in a single day's fishing.

Normal drift fishing is impossible, for the prevailing current sweeps any boat rapidly over and away from the top of the bank. Local practice is to anchor over the ridge, using a huge block of stone as an anchor weight. This stone is attached to a marker buoy which is kept inside the boat until a fish is hooked. The buoy is then slid rapidly over the side, leaving the boat free to follow a hooked fish. Once the fish has been successfully boated the skipper then takes his boat back to the buoy and ties it up to the anchor line. In this way it is possible to fish in the same 'chum' line throughout the day.

On this particular day fortune was with me and I had started well. I had one 200 pound blue shark already in the boat and within minutes of re-starting had a take from a cruising blue shark which had circled our boat several times before accepting the bait. As I've already said, blue shark are seldom strong fighters and this fish was no exception. Later, on boating it, we discovered that the fish had lost half of its upper tail lobe. Earlier on, when the blue shark had been some twenty yards from the boat, we saw a big yellow-brown form ease up behind it. Although obviously a shark of some kind, the second fish was too far away from us for positive identification. In comparison to the ultra-slim form of the hooked blue, this second shark looked thick-set and bulky. Twice it made an attack on the blue shark, and on both occasions the hooked fish crammed on speed in an attempt to avoid its aggressor.

It was not long before I was able to bring the hooked fish into gaffing range and, at this stage, the second, mysterious shark vanished. Similar in size to the first blue shark already in the boat, this second one pleased me greatly: and with more than half a day's fishing still left to go, I had hopes that this would be something of a red-letter day.

The distance from the point where we had boated the blue shark back to the buoyed anchor line was close to a mile. With this in mind I certainly did not expect to see the other shark again, but within ten minutes of re-starting fishing a great yellow-brown shadow passed swiftly under our boat and surfaced to push idly at the balloon float. (I was later to discover that white tip, like porbeagle shark, have a playful streak which draws them to make mock attacks on floating objects.)

At this stage it was easy to see the new shark clearly. Tiny eyes, great broad, flat snout and a huge rounded dorsal fin tipped distinctly in off-white. Closer inspection showed us the same white tips to the pectoral fins.

'White tip', I shouted.

My skipper, Francisco Van Uden had never seen one of these fish before, although he had read about them. Quite obviously, we both badly wanted to get this fish into the boat: both as a sporting species and to set a new European record. Gently winding the line back in, I pulled the balloon float away from the shark and slowly worked the bait back towards the surface. Finally, with the float removed from the line, I had the big bait – a whole red bream – stationed twenty feet back from the boat at a depth of around twelve to fifteen feet.

The big shark had vanished when I first moved the bait and float. Now it re-appeared, not in an obvious way but as a dark shadow in the water well below the bait. Time and again it vanished, only to flit briefly back into view, either below or behind the bait. The fish was hungry, that much was obvious. It was stalking the bait but lacked the confidence to make its final attack. This is something I have had happen with many species of shark, and I knew from past experience that if I dropped the bait back I might just induce the fish to feed.

Picking up the rod, I pushed the 10-0 reel into free spool and with just my thumb as a brake I let the bait float back and down away from the boat.

Ten, twenty, thirty yards of line ran off the big reel spool when, almost imperceptibly, I felt a slight bump on the line.

So slight was this that at first I thought I had imagined it. Then, slowly but dramatically, the 130 class dacron line began to pull off the reel and I knew for certain that the huge shark had the bait in its jaws.

This first run from a shark is always one of the most exciting and exhilarating aspects of shark fishing. Still with my reel in free spool I watched and waited for the first savage rush to end. When the fish did stop I quickly estimated that I had lost a further 40 or so yards of line, which meant that the white tip was approximately 80 to 90 yards from the boat.

At this stage – with the fish stationary – I put the big reel into gear, made a quick adjustment to the drag and then watched for the fish to move off on its second and highly critical run. A mistake now would cost me the fish and I badly wanted everything to work well.

Behind me the crew of the boat watched in total silence. They all knew how I felt, and they all waited heart in mouth for the slack line between rod and sea to draw tight. As always, I sensed the forward motion of the fish before I saw my line begin to move. Bracing myself for the impact to come, I waited while the line drew taut and then, as the weight of the fish drew the rod tip down and round, I leaned back and struck as hard as I dared.

One strike was enough. The moment that fish felt the hook it took off in a bull-like rush, tearing yards and yards of line off the reel spool. At the time I was unaware of a sudden burst of activity behind me: I had my own problems. The main one of which was to get safely into the fighting chair. Never an easy task, I had the additional hazard of manoeuvring round two dead blue shark to overcome. Everything went well, however, and as I sat down in the fighting chair I heard the big boat's engine's roar into life and knew that Francisco was backing away from the big anchor buoy.

The first few minutes of the fight were as always a problem. Big shark are far from stupid and – like so many other shark I have caught – this one made straight for the buoyed anchor rope. I knew and I am sure the shark knew that once my dacron line touched the wire-taut anchor rope my line would part as though it had been slashed by a knife. Thankfully I was able to turn the huge fish with a few yards to spare and as it swung away and down I knew that barring the hook-hold slipping or some similar unforeseen disaster, I would ultimately put that fish into the boat.

Despite its slow moving appearance I soon discovered that the fish was capable of showing a good turn of speed. Having not caught white tip previously, I was not sure what to expect in terms of fight but knowing the ways of shark I fully expected fireworks at some stage of the battle. I found out soon enough that the white tip has its own distinctive style of fighting. Unlike many other species of shark which rely only on speed, the white tip uses a mixture of speed and savage head shaking. So powerful was this head-shaking routine that on each occasion I was suddenly lifted part of the way out of the fighting chair. A bout of head shaking was nearly always followed instantly by a fast, powerful run. My estimate of size on this fish was around 200 or so pounds. Not a big fish, I thought, but not a small one either.

At that stage of the game I did not realise that white tip of this size were in the record breaking class. The fish was too big to bully, even on the heavy 130 pound class gear that I was using. Not that this worried me. I had plenty of time and my intention was to catch the white tip even if it took all day. All of us in that boat wanted the opportunity to examine the shark closely, both in the boat when it was gaffed and back on the island.

Constant pressure finally took its toll, and it didn't take much more than twenty minutes hard fighting to bring a very tired shark alongside for gaffing. With two gaffs firmly set inside its mouth and its big tail securely roped down, our next step was to physically heave the huge fish into the boat.

Unlike blue shark, which are long, slim and evenly proportioned, white tip are top heavy creatures. Most of a white tip's weight is centred in its broad head and wide shoulders, and in this case catching it proved to be easier than heaving it into the boat. Finally, however, it crashed down into the cockpit, snapping its vast jaws wildly at anything within range. Luckily for everyone there the only thing that got damaged was a gaff handle, which was snapped into several sections.

We were now ready to go in and weigh up the fish at the

dockside. On the homeward journey, which took nearly three hours, we had ample time and opportunity to inspect the fish, paying particular attention to its tiny snake-like eyes, immensely broad jaw and formidable row of close-set teeth.

I knew from reading books on shark that the white tip was an oceanic species; common in tropical seas; said to be the commonest large animal on earth (large in this case meaning over a hundred pounds in weight); a known man-eater; and generally reckoned to be a school shark.

I also remembered seeing a film entitled *Blue Water White Death,* a factual account of hunting for great white shark. Part of the film had been shot on the whaling grounds off South Africa, and in one sequence a pack of white tip shark made life very uncomfortable for the cameramen. So much so, that the film team were finally forced to vacate the area.

Out of the water, the white tip we had taken certainly looked formidable. Huge jaw muscles made its face even broader, evidence that this fish had tremendous biting ability. Obviously a tough customer, I began wondering how and why this one happened to be so far from its normal habitat.

Back at the dock the fish weighed in at 211 pounds. On the trip back it had obviously lost a lot of weight, and if weighed when caught would have tipped the scales at around 240-250 pounds. Weight loss in caught fish is inevitable and as the shark was without question a European record no one was worried about the lost poundage.

The interesting thing for me was the reaction from the local professional fishermen. All of them knew the local shark types well; yet none had ever seen this particular species before in local waters. Of the dozens of fishermen I talked to, only one – a man from the Cape Verde Islands – knew the fish. He had seen them in Cape Verde where, he said, they were known as *tibbuna & pana na costa da Africa* (the sharks from the coast of Africa).

Naturally, we all assumed my fish to be a stray. The next day, however, while fishing in the same locality we had seven white tip shark in sight at one time. The previous day's fish was obviously part of a school of white tip that was using the fish-rich Condor Bank as a well stocked larder. Of the seven we saw during the course of that second day, I hooked four, boated two, and lost two due to the line being cut by other shark. There was not much I could do about such losses. The problem was simply that as soon as I hooked a fish, the other white tips attracted by the hooked shark's unusual behaviour would follow it closely, with the result that my line would pass over or round their rough bodies; the skin of all shark is covered in tiny denticles – each one sharp enough to cut through a taut line.

I had to leave Fayal shortly afterwards and it was not until September of the next year that I went back. Again we fished shark on the Condor Bank and the talk on the first day was all of white tip shark . . . was the fishing of the previous season a fluke? A chance encounter with a band of wandering fish well off course from their normal feeding grounds?

We had our answer within minutes of anchoring. I had hardly put a bait over the side before a hefty white tip cruised under the boat and picked up the bait. From that time on we sighted white tip shark on each occasion we fished the bank. Again I got a record. Beating my previous season's best by 4.5 pounds to take the record weight up to 215 pounds.

By now I had gleaned from my fishing much additional information about white tip over the Condor Bank. I knew that the average Azores' fish was around seven feet in length: at the upper-end of the known size for white tip shark. Scientists had heard of fish of up to nine or even twelve feet but no one had as yet secured a specimen of this size and most of the white tip caught elsewhere measured between four and six feet: which meant that these Fayal fish were giants in comparison.

The following year, in August 1982, I returned to Fayal Island, intending to stay there fishing until the middle of the second week in September. I was approximately three weeks earlier in arriving than on my visits for the two previous years. Those three weeks made a big difference. I fished the Condor Bank on a number of occasions, taking some fine blue shark and several high-jumping mako in the process, but at no time did I see a white tip. During the first week in September I was joined by an old friend of mine, angling journalist Jens Ploug Hansen from Denmark who arrived wanting to catch mako: something he achieved on his first day.

Then, on my last fishing day off the Island, a hefty white tip surfaced directly astern of our boat. The fish was hungry but shy. It looked huge, far larger than my own record fish of the two previous seasons. We were using some very high, minced bonito as 'chum' and this had obviously attracted and was holding the shark's attention. Time and again the enormous white tip would follow a bait in towards the boat, but on each occasion it turned away without taking. Jens finally wound in his line, removed his freshbait and attached a great fillet of very, very smelly bonito! This time the white tip did not even hesitate.

Within seconds it was hooked and Jens was fighting it as hard as he dared on a 50 pound class outfit. On the light rig, the shark showed no inclination to run. It simply took up a position approximately 40 yards astern of our boat and stayed in sight for the major part of the ensuing battle. Finally, it was alongside us where it was rapidly gaffed, tail roped and physically dragged inboard. Once in the boat it looked larger than ever, and I was convinced that Jens had broken my two previous records.

It was not to be. The fish, a female with a huge head and jaws, was something of an optical illusion. Its actual weight was 204 pounds, well under the weight of my world-record fish, but even so, it was a line-class record: the largest white tip shark ever caught on 50 pound class tackle. And Jens Ploug Hansen was naturally pleased. I too was happy, about both the fish Jens had taken and the fact that for the third year in succession white tip shark had appeared off the Azores.

September was definitely the month that white tips arrived in Azorian waters, which accounted for why they had never been seen by the local commercial fishermen. Most local boats either bottom fish or troll for tuna and September normally marks the end of a season's fishing. So the reason no one had seen white tips before was, quite possibly, that no boats had fished the offshore marks after the first week of that month. Catching fish once over the bank could be coincidental, but taking similar fish three years in a row indicated that white tip shark migrate annually to the Azores area.

This means that yet another large sporting species can now be listed for European waters. This is important. The records

I have already established for this species are, obviously, made to be broken and I hope this is exactly what will happen, as increased game angling activity around the Azores comes to mean greater opportunity for anglers to fish specifically for shark of record size. In my estimation the white tip shark record could eventually be broken by a fish of somewhere between 300 and 450 pounds. And I have certainly hooked and lost, or seen white tip shark in this weight range.

As a new big game species, the white tip in European waters is an exciting discovery. White tips may not have the speed or aerobatic ability of the mako shark, but they do have enough strength and tenacity to put them high on the list of sporting fish.

Hammerhead Shark

One of the largest hammerhead sharks I ever encountered was a huge specimen that I hooked in August 1982 while fishing 40 miles south of Pico in the Azores.

At the time the boat was anchored on the edge of the Azores Bank itself. Always a fine fishing area, this bank is known to hold big fish of many kinds. Tuna, swordfish and a variety of big sharks all use the bank as a larder, and on this day we hoped to entice one or other species to feed, as the weather was good with a slight breeze from the southwest, making fishing conditions perfect, particularly for shark or swordfish.

Within minutes of anchoring, a huge manta ray appeared and began slowly to circle our boat. It looked to have a wing span of at least 12 feet. Manta ray never take bait but, even so, it was fascinating to be given the opportunity to study such a huge creature at close range. So close to us did the fish come that for a while it was impossible to run out our lines without standing the chance of foulhooking the giant fish. So we had to wait until it abandoned its endless circling of our boat and vanished from sight.

At this stage I put out two rods, both baited with live sea bream. One bait was set at 10 fathoms (60 feet). The other at over 60 fathoms (360 feet). By setting the baits at such varied depths I hoped to attract a swordfish to the deep set bait and a shark to the near surface bait. As always, a mesh bag full of mashed fish and fish oil was hung over the side to spread a 'smell lane' which would attract fish, particularly shark, to the boat.

Soon after putting the mesh bag over, the bait set at 60 fathoms was taken by a very, very large fish. Initially I hoped for swordfish but soon realised that the culprit was a giant six gilled shark. These deep water shark grow to weights in excess of two thousand pounds. Fish of a thousand pounds being regarded as an average specimen! This one felt huge and I knew that, as always happened, it would ultimately turn and head down at speed for the sea bed. Sure enough, within minutes the shark turned and began its final run. I tried piling on pressure to slow down or stop the huge fish but as is usual it simply increased its rate of descent until my line parted under the strain.

I have hooked and lost a number of six gilled shark over the years, always in this way. To the best of my knowledge only one six gilled shark has ever been caught on rod and line. It was taken off Madeira and weighed 1,475 pounds. Once these six gilled shark start to feed, it then becomes a waste of everyone's time, line and end tackle to put baits down deep. Six gilled shark appear to be a pack fish and where one is hooked you can usually find plenty more.

To avoid this I tied on a new trace, attached a large livebait to the hook and set the tackle at 15 fathoms (90 feet). More mashed fish was then added to the rubby dubby bag and I settled back prepared to wait for results. Within minutes my brief wait was over. A very, very large hammerhead charged the boat in an attempt to snatch our rubby dubby bag and, at one stage, it looked as though the shark would actually jump into the boat's cockpit. Twice the hammerhead reared right out of the water, crashing heavily against the boat's transom. Each time it reared, its vast hammer-like head protruded above the transom – just as though the shark was attempting to size-up the occupants of the cockpit – and at no time did the fish show fear.

The behaviour of this hammerhead was abnormal. Few sharks show much fear of a boat, but not even the mighty mako makes the sort of attack that this one was attempting. I

have seen a hooked shark crash into a boat but never have I
seen a fresh, unhooked fish behave in such a frenzied and
frightening way. Again and again the shark tried for our
dangling rubby dubby. Each time either I or the skipper
managed to snatch it away.

By this stage the huge hammerhead was sweeping round
our stern in tight, angry circles. Twice I tempted it with
livebaits, twice it inspected and rejected the baits. Then on the
third pass it rushed the bait, its jaws agape, its tail lashing the
sea's surface to foam. But despite this great show of ferocity it
turned aside at the last possible second, passing so close that its
broad head actually picked up the trace in passing.

For a terrible moment I thought the great fish had
foulhooked itself, which was the last thing I wanted. This was
a record breaker if I ever saw one: the European record and
perhaps the world record was there for the taking and I did not
want the fish foulhooked. A situation which would
immediately eliminate the fish from any record claim.

I was certain that baited correctly this fish would feed, so in
came one set of tackle for re-baiting. The succulent – and to
my eyes tempting – livebait was replaced with a whole but
very long-dead bonito. This fish was so rotten with
decomposition that the only place a hook would hold was in
the bait's bony head structure. Dropping this new bait
overboard I watched as it began to sink. Behind it stretched a
trail of rusty-coloured blood and oil, which seeped away into
the otherwise clear water.

The patrolling hammerhead obviously saw the bait the
moment it hit the water, for less than a trace-length down the
mighty fish crashed into the rotten bait with such speed and
power that the rotting flesh disintegrated, and for a brief
moment the shark's whole broad head vanished in a cloud of
putrescent matter. Then the fish was off at high speed. The
very second my line began to leave the screaming reel I noticed
that where the trace-swivel joined the double reel line there
was one solitary turn of dacron line round the wire. Frankly I
felt ill. I knew that the moment I struck the taut line would
part on impact. My only hope was that, as the line ran out, the
one tiny loop would manage to clear itself before the fibre line
became damaged – but my luck was out.

As I pushed the reel into gear and braced myself for impact the huge fish reared itself half out of the water in a violent welter of white spray. As the fish came up I clearly saw the line part and I knew that the huge fish was gone for good. Fisherman's luck of the worst kind. Losing a shark of this calibre sickened us all.

We waited twenty minutes just in case the fish was stupid enough to come back. Blue shark that have been lost occasionally sweep back to take a second bait and hook, but not this hammerhead. Two giant fish – the six gill and the hammerhead – lost in a single day was more than enough for us and we started back on the three-hour journey to the harbour at Horta.

This was simply a case of very bad luck, for I have caught plenty of other large hammerhead, mostly on trolled baits. Hammerheads are highly active and aggressive fish, and when in a feeding mood they will attack anything of edible size which moves through the water.

Once I even took a good-sized hammerhead on a bait which consisted of two head-hooked flatfish, mounted white belly side out for maximum flash in the water (see Fig. 16). This was a desperation bait, used in most unusual circumstances but it proved effective. I had been fishing all day and had taken a

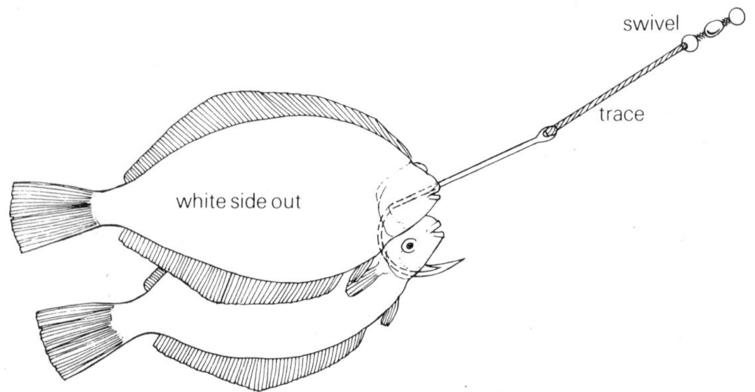

FIGURE 16   Although unusual, two flatfish white side out once hooked me a beautiful hammerhead shark. No matter how poor or unusual a bait looks its appearance changes when it is moved away from a hunting fish!

400 pound mako on conventional tackle. On our return trip to harbour a large dorsal fin was sighted and – as we cruised up to the fish – it became obvious that it was a good-sized hammerhead shark. On this occasion, my crew had never baited for a hammerhead before and they assumed that a static bait would be best. I argued against this technique, saying I wanted to troll a bait around and in front of the cruising shark. The only baits we had left, however, were two diminutive flatfish but 'nothing ventured nothing gained'! On they went, hooked once through the head. As I paid out line the skipper turned his boat to bring the wildly flashing bait passed the shark's great nose. Nothing, not a flicker of a fin nor a single movement to show that the hammerhead had sighted the bait. However, the next pass was different. As the double bait passed in front of its nose, the shark eased forward and started slowly to follow the lure.

Quickly signalling to the skipper to speed up, I started to draw the bait away from the shark. A hunting shark always hates to lose a meal and this fish was no exception. Each time the boat's speed increased, the shark increased its tail beat until the fish was streaking along leaving a wide, white wake behind it.

I knew then that nothing would deter the fish. Waiting until the right second, I threw the reel out of gear to drop the bait right back on its nose. Instinctively the shark opened its mouth and I saw the double-bait vanish into a very impressive maw. Striking was a formality. I simply pushed the reel into gear and let the forward motion of the boat and the weight of the shark set the hook.

Hammerhead shark are capable of attaining great speed despite their misleadingly lethargic appearance. The moment it felt the hook that fish went into a savage crash dive, which ripped several hundred yards of line off the reel. This was interesting fishing. I was using a 50 pound class outfit on a fish which subsequently weighed in at over 250 pounds. That first dive was hard to stop. The fish had deep water beneath it and every intention of reaching safety on the bottom some 500 yards down. Initially the lightish rod simply bent to the shark's movements but even something as comparatively light as a 50 pound class outfit has a tremendous ability to tame big fish, and at a little over 200 yards the fish was obviously taking more punishment than it could handle.

A big fish fighting at such depths has many advantages over the angler. Its own strength and fighting ability, coupled with water pressure, can easily break a light line. To counteract both factors the angler is forced to slacken his reel drag considerably. Under these conditions, big fish experience is invaluable and I found myself instinctively taking all the steps essential to avoid a breakage.

For a while the fish and I slogged it out. Not taking or giving line. Simply fighting in a fixed area. Then, and only then, did I begin to pile on pressure. Gaining a yard or two of line only to lose it again on the next downward plunge of the hooked shark.

Finally I managed to start the fish circling, and soon after I began to bring it up. Only a yard or two at a time, but as the line began to build up on my reel spool I knew that – barring unforeseen accidents – I would bring that fish to the gaff. Within twenty minutes the shark was in clear view spiralling up out of the depths to arrive totally exhausted on the surface. Gaffing was easy. The fish showed absolutely no sign of fight even when the skipper slipped the tail ropes over the hammerhead's mighty tail fin.

A nice shark on an unusual bait: a bait which only worked because it had been fished on the troll. No matter how poor a bait looks, its appearance changes when it is moved away from the hunting fish. A hammerhead which turns up its nose at a stationary bait will almost certainly charge a bait that moves, even if the moving bait is a pair of tiny flatfish.

Giant Skate Fishing

Common skate – sometimes known as grey or blue skate – grow to huge weights. Specimens up to 150 pound are still comparatively common and fish of 200 pound plus are known to exist in many places off the coast of Britain and Ireland. Under favourable conditions, individual skate reach weights in excess of 300 pounds, and one commercially-caught fish weighed in at 400 pounds and over 7 feet in length. Although not technically a true big game species, giant skate are large and powerful enough to attract the attention of many big fish anglers.

Twenty years ago giant skate were common in many waters. Nowadays, over exploitation by anglers and by commercial fishing interests has considerably reduced the giant skate population, and the best giant skate fishing grounds are now confined to cold northern waters.

The real 'hotspot' marks these days are Strangford Lough (Northern Ireland), the Isle of Mull, the Orkneys and the Shetland Isles. Anglers from all over Europe make regular pilgrimages to these areas, often with spectacular results. I have been fortunate enough to fish all of these venues and have had skate in excess of 150 pounds from each locality.

Tackle

Rods

Despite its huge size and obvious strength a giant skate does not make long runs like a shark or halibut. Occasionally, a fish will move off strongly but for most of the time a skate will be content to fight directly beneath the boat. Because of this skate can be caught on reasonably light tackle. I once had a 150 pounder from the Isle of Mull on a 30 pound IGFA rod and line of 30 pound breaking strain. This fish was taken from a depth of just over 200 feet and took no more than ten minutes to subdue. Even so, I feel in retrospect that the rod I used was a little tc light for skate fishing.

My preference is for a matched 50 pound class outfit. There are many of these on the market and all are suitable for giant skate fishing. Mv own skate rods are fitted with a full set of AFTCO roller rings. To cut costs however, a rod fitted with a roller butt and tip will work just as well. Roller guides are essential if wire lines are to be used.

Reels

The most suitable reels for big skate fishing are the Penn 6-0 and the Tatler V reel. Of the two I prefer the Tatler, but both reels hold plenty of line and both are designed for hard work.

Lines

A nylon or dacron (polyester fibre) line can be used for normal fishing conditions. My preference with skate is for dacron. This is thinner than nylon of the same breaking strain, and therefore it offers less resistance to the tide flow. As always the only slight disadvantage to dacron is its lack of elasticity. Nylon will stretch amazingly well under strain but dacron does not, which allows little leeway for mistakes when playing a big fish. Correct use of the reel's star-drag breaking system is essential if lost fish are to be avoided. Wire line can be used in heavy tide areas. Wire has the advantage of being ultra fine, with its own built in weight factor – something that allows the angler to fish comfortably in strong tides – its disadvantages are a tendency to kink and a total lack of elasticity. However, I think its advantage outweighs its disadvantages.

Choosing a wire line is not always that easy, as at least three types of line are available. Single strand stainless steel, braided wire and *monel* metal wire. All have disadvantages. The single strand wire has a tendency to kink and then part under pressure; the braided wire is less inclined to kink but soon frays with regular use; while the monel metal is thicker than the other two types of wire and less pleasant to use. Despite this, monel metal wire is the most reliable of the three and so I would recommend it to anyone contemplating wire line fishing.

Traces

Many anglers use traces of nylon covered line for big skate fishing. Personally I prefer to make my own skate traces from heavy nylon. As skate do not have teeth – although their lips carry bony plates, which can chafe and crush – I find that heavy 'long line' nylon can easily withstand the rigours of skate fishing. The suppleness of the nylon also makes for better bait presentation. I normally make my skate traces 24 inches long. This is long enough, for large skate are seldom tackle shy and seem to ignore the close proximity of a lead weight.

Hooks

As already stated, skate are large heavy fish with big mouths, so the hook you use will have to take a great deal of strain. Never use cheap hooks; it isn't worth the aggravation of having one snap under pressure. The ideal big skate hook is a size 8-0 or 10-0 Mustad Seamaster pattern. Mustad O'Shaugnessy hooks are also very strong and reliable. Both patterns should be carefully sharpened before use.

Avoid the American-style eagle claw hooks, as these have long and excessively brittle points. I have seen far too many large fish lost with this style of hook, and in all cases the hook snapped off just by the barb.

Location and Methods

Giant skate – like most big fish – tend to pick out a section of food-rich sea bed and take up permanent residence in this comparatively small area. Although not a shoal fish, a number of individual specimens may live in close harmony. This means that it is often possible to catch a number of large skate in a single day's fishing.

In my experience skate show a distinct preference for ground that is situated close to a main run of tide, as a heavy tide flow will provide the waiting fish with a plentiful supply of food. When fishing within Strangford Lough, in Northern Ireland, was still popular, one of the major hotspots was a mark directly between two closely spaced islands. This hole only fished on an ebb tide, when the strong tide flow syphoned out of the upper lough. The giant skate all came from an area of slack water on the very edge of the tide run (see Fig. 17). The best specimen out of this hole was a magnificent 181 pound fish.

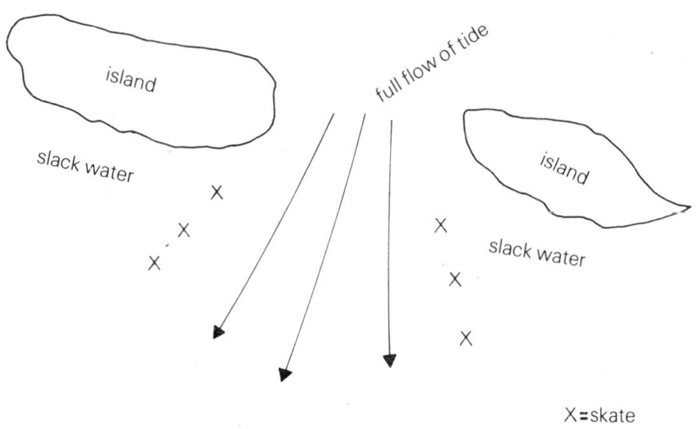

FIGURE 17   Skate prefer slack water on the edge of a main run of tide, where the flow of water can provide them with a plentiful supply of food. A gap between islands provides an ideal site.

In Scapa Flow, on Orkney, one of the best skate marks of all lies at a point directly behind an island. The tide race is split by this island, once again leaving an area of slack water in which numerous skate congregate (see Fig. 18). My personal best

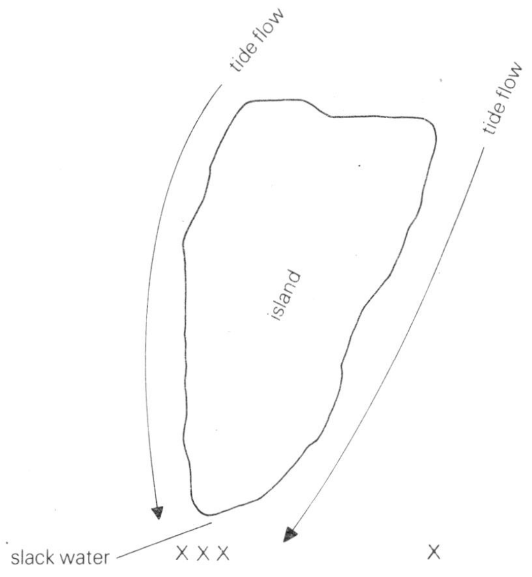

FIGURE 18   Typical skate habitat. A tidal flow split by an island provides a slack area for skate to congregate.

fish from this area weighed 158 pounds and on the same day I took a second fish weighing exactly 150 pounds, then lost a third large skate when the hook pulled out during the first few minutes of the battle.

The largest common skate I have caught to date was also an Orkney fish. Unlike most of the other huge skate from Orkney this one was not caught in Scapa Flow. Instead it came from a mark situated about five miles from Kirkwall Harbour. Boatman Eddie Sinclair – a well-known local figure – had told me that local scallop divers had spotted some large skate patrolling a deep yet sheltered hole situated in the lee of a rugged headland. On looking at a sea chart of the area I could see instantly that this mark was typical of the preferred skate habitat. The tide which swept through between two islands was deflected by the headland, leaving an area of fairly slack water with a uniform depth of between 90 and 100 feet. This area was rich in scallops, and as scallops form a major part of the diet of big skate, the mark obviously had great, although as yet undiscovered, potential.

Having discussed the mark with Eddie Sinclair, I booked his boat for the next day and kept my fingers crossed for good weather. The weather turned out to be quite reasonable – overcast with a little rain but thankfully no wind. We timed our arrival for an hour before the slack-tide period and our idea was to fish right through the flood tide, when the flow could be expected to bring food directly to the lurking skate. On the way to the mark we had stopped twice to catch fresh bait. Big skate will take most kinds of fish – including smaller skate – but show a preference for fresh coalfish. Luckily the coalfish (or *laythe* as they are called locally) were in great abundance and it didn't take us long to catch a dozen or more three-quarter pound fish for bait.

On arrival at the mark we dropped our anchor so that the boat would lie right on the edge of the tide flow. With the boat settled, I made up my tackle, baited with a good-sized freshly-caught laythe and began to fish. We did not expect much action during the slack water period and, as we suspected, nothing occurred until the tide had started to run at full speed. I checked the bait once, during this waiting period, to make sure that it was not being eaten by crabs or the ever present whelks, but neither scavenger had been at the bait so down it went again hopefully to attract a large skate.

Twenty minutes later there was a gentle pluck at the rod tip, and I knew that a hundred feet beneath our keel a skate had located my bait and was, I hoped, sucking the baited laythe into its great mouth. Twice more the rod tip nodded gently and then my line fell slack as the great fish swam back up the tide (strangely enough nearly all the large skate I have ever caught or seen caught have moved up against the tide soon after taking the bait).

Hooking a large skate is simply a matter of taking up the slack line, then striking as soon as the weight of the moving fish is felt. This fish reacted the moment my hook was set. Unlike most skate I have had, this one made no attempt to settle back on the sea bed. Instead it turned in a half circle and made a long, fast run down tide.

The trick when playing a giant skate is to keep its nose up, so that the full flow of tidal pressure forces the great flat body of the skate up towards the surface. If the fish is allowed to get its head down and flop back to the sea bed the suction created by its saucer-like body makes it extremely difficult to play out. In this case increased rod pressure brought the skate spiralling slowly up. I knew, however, that the moment it saw the light it would turn and crash dive at full speed. Time and time again I have seen anglers smashed by this manoeuvre, and I have learnt always to slacken the reel drag a fraction as the fish comes up.

Sure enough, the fish came to within about twenty feet of the surface, took fright and dived. It is surprising how much speed a big skate can show when it is badly frightened. This one ripped line from off the big reel, and had I not eased the drag slightly a breakage would have been certain. Luckily for me I was able to slow its rate of descent fairly quickly, and so managed to prevent the skate from making contact with the sea bed. Thwarted in its dive for safety the fish then decided to put as much distance between itself and the boat as possible.

I had not yet seen the fish but I knew from its strength and movements that it was very big indeed, possibly in excess of 200 pounds. So when it took off on this second run I already knew I had a longish fight on my hands. To begin with the fish took line fast and steadily then, with about 100 yards of line out, it settled in to the normal surging fight-style so typical of big skate. Once again my problem was to stop the fish seeking refuge on the sea bed. With that amount of line out, I knew I would never be able to prise it loose if it reached the bottom, so I began to pile on the pressure. Slowly but surely I turned the fish up and back towards the boat. This time I knew from the fish's response that if I could get it to the surface I would be able to bring the great skate alongside for gaffing. Pumping up any big fish is always hard work, and this one was no exception. However I was able to gain line steadily and within five minutes the fish was in sight: a vast triangular shape, hanging two yards under the surface directly behind the boat's transom. For a moment or two I could not get the fish to move, then by increasing the rod pressure almost to breaking point I felt the creature ease forward just a fraction, and once on the move it glided up easily.

Apparently exhausted, it came alongside in a perfect position for gaffing. Skipper Sinclair simply reached over the side and snicked the gaff hook firmly into the huge wing. As he started to lift the fish, I saw the hook of the stainless steel gaff begin to straighten out. A second later the gaff slipped from its hold and in a sudden burst of activity the giant fish thrashed the water to foam as it took off on its strongest run of the fight. Fortunately as soon as the fish was gaffed I had once again followed my normal habit of slackening the reel drag, just in case the skate decided to prolong the battle. This precaution was the only reason my line didn't snap instantly. I was still in trouble, however, for the fish took off more than 50 yards of line and then stopped moving, to take up a position directly under the surface. Although the skate was obviously exhausted, it would soon regain its strength given a little rest. My problem was that due to line angle I could not apply more than holding pressure, and there was absolutely no possibility of pumping the fish back.

I had been in this position once before, and knew that my only hope was to drift the boat back to the fish. I quickly explained my plan to the skipper and within seconds he was paying out rope so that the boat dropped back. Everything went well, and as we drifted into gaffing range I dropped the rod, picked up a huge gaff, and drove it firmly into the skate's vast wing. Within seconds, the skipper had a second gaff firmly embedded and the giant fish was ours. Back in Kirkwall that evening the skate weighed in at 192 pounds. Not my hoped-for 200 pounder, but still a very big skate and a personal best for the species.

Giant Skate Conservation

Like most anglers fishing over the last few decades I have been guilty of needlessly killing big skate. Large skate are of no use to man as a food fish, and most of those caught by anglers are killed, photographed and ultimately dumped back in the sea when they begin to decompose.

Fortunately conservation of this species is now widely practised and there are signs that giant skate are beginning to re-establish themselves in many areas. In one such area, off Tobermory on the Isle of Mull, local charter boat skipper Brian Swinbanks has brought the art of 'catch and return' to perfection.

Skipper Swinbanks knows a great deal about big skate and insists that each fish caught from his boat is weighed and then returned alive. To achieve this he has fitted a special gantry to the side of his wheelhouse. Played-out skate are brought alongside and gaffed in the wing. The gaff hook is then transferred to the gantry rope and scales, and the fish is hauled directly out of the water, weighed, photographed, and with the minimum delay swung back over the side and released.

Skate are tough fish and the insertion of the gaff hook into the edge of a wing does little or no harm. I have fished on several occasions with Brian Swinbanks and each time giant skate have been taken. On my last trip I had a 150 pound specimen. Proof that his lifting equipment can handle very big fish.

Tuna Fishing

Throughout the waters of the world there are many, many species of tuna. In European waters, however, we are more limited in opportunity, although the tuna tribe is still well represented. From the fisherman's point of view tuna can be arranged into two obvious categories – large and small. The large variety comprise the blue fin tuna, which can reach weights of 1,000 pounds or more. The smaller variety range in weight from 60 pounds up to just over 400 pounds. Irrespective of species, all tuna are unusually strong fighters, easily capable of making long downward runs when hooked and putting up a prolonged battle. For this reason light tackle should not be used.

Unfortunately for anglers, the blue fin and the big eyed tuna tend to intermingle. Although they do not shoal together, when large concentrations of bait fish are located both species will probably be present in the area. This is another reason for using heavy tackle.

Tackle

Rods

In my opinion, only two weights of rod are suitable for catching tuna. These are the 80 pound class and the 130 pound class IGFA rated rods. The 80 pound class is perfectly adequate for tuna up to 400 pounds but for fish over this weight the 130 pound class rod is the most suitable.

Light tackle enthusiasts will probably protest that such rods are little more than clothes poles. The thing to remember, however, is that tuna in European waters are invariably caught over very deep water. This allows them to fight at full capacity. In the USA and off Canada, where tuna fishing is very popular, most large tuna are caught in water of less than one hundred feet in depth. Shallow water tuna are rarely able to put up a prolonged struggle, and many giant blue fins are brought to the gaff in a matter of minutes rather than hours. This is not so in European waters. In the Azores, for example, a Swedish angler fought a large blue fin for nine and a half hours. At the end of this period the fish was still going strong when the line parted. For European tuna fishing then, rods of under an 80 pounds class rating are not recommended.

Reels

Tuna are big hard-fighting fish that test all fishing equipment beyond reasonable tolerances. For this reason only top quality reels should be used when tuna fishing. There are now numerous makes of reel on the market, many of these of Far Eastern origin. Most look good value but none compare with reels like the Fin-Nor, the Penn International or the tried and trusted Penn Senator range.

The Senator with its old fashioned drag system may appear to be crude in comparison to the lever drag Fin-Nor or Penn International but its internal gearing system has been tried, tested and approved on hundreds of thousands of giant fish. The Senator then, is the perfect reel for an angler who has to watch the finances. However, if money is no object then the Fin-Nor, the Penn International or the new Zane Grey reels from Hardys must be the obvious choice.

The newly introduced Zane Grey range has already produced a number of record fish, including a magnificent blue marlin (Hawaii) of over 1,600 pounds.

Lines

Big game anglers have divided opinions on lines. Some like dacron, while others prefer monofilament. Both lines have their advantages and disadvantages. Once hooked, large tuna dive deep. When this occurs monofilament lines are inclined to stretch to such an extent that it is difficult to pull with the full weight on the fish. Dacron, on the other hand, is largely stretch free, which allows the angler to apply maximum pressure to a hooked tuna. But the drawback to dacron becomes apparent when other large fish swim into the taut line, which promptly parts to release the hooked fish. This is a common accident with shoal fish like tuna. Monofilament also contracts on the reel spool when wound back under heavy pressure, and this contraction can easily distort a metal spool.

Most makes of reel claim that this distortion does not occur but experienced big game anglers can quote instances of this happening. In the end line choice is up to individual preference. In my own case I prefer the dacron line, despite the occasional loss of a fish 'cut off' by other tuna.

Traces

Tuna have hard but toothless mouths. Because of this, wire traces are not needed. Heavy duty 'long line' nylon makes the perfect material for a tuna trace. I use nylon with a breaking strain of 300 pounds.

Hooks

For live or dead bait fishing I use 10-0 or 12-0 Seamaster hooks from Mustad (Norway). I have tried many other types but have yet to find a better pattern than the Seamaster.

Lures

Once feeding, tuna will hit just about any type of lure. The favourite lure, however, is the Japanese feather (see Fig. 19). Although these come in a wide range of colours and weights, the most useful weight is the 8-12 ounce range. Tuna would also appear to have colour preferences. Big eye tuna seem to take mainly red and white lures, while blue fin prefer all black, or green and yellow lures.

All types of Kona Head lures (see Fig. 19) attract and catch tuna. Where possible it helps to match the rubber skirt colours to the bait fish present in the feeding area. For example, when tuna are feeding on mackerel, blue and silver should be used

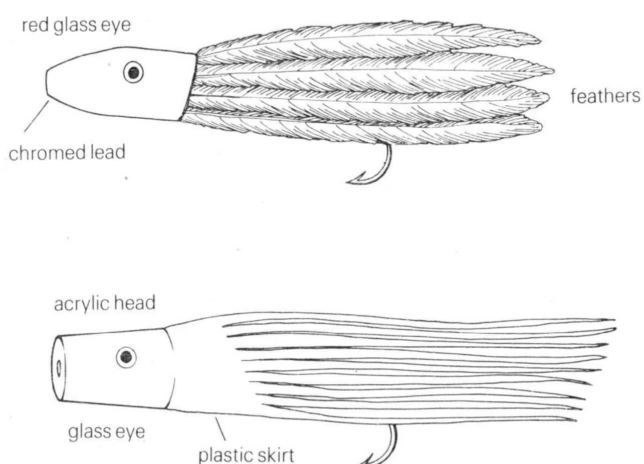

FIGURE 19 'Japanese feather' lures are spectacularly successful as baits for tuna (as are Kona Head lures). Colours used should be matched to the tuna species. Big eye seem to prefer red and white lures, while blue fin prefer lures that are green and yellow, or all black.

on the lure. If small dorado are the quarry, then green and yellow or blue and yellow are the colours to choose.

When squid are the predominant food then pink and black is best. An agitated squid often turns pink and begins to throw out black ink, so the pink and black skirts of the Kona Head simulate the colours of a badly frightened squid, which may well fool a hunting tuna into striking at the artificial bait.

Location and Methods

In the days when the North Sea held numerous blue fin tuna the accepted angling method was to drift fish from a small boat controlled by an oarsman. The technique was simple. Handfuls of herring or mackerel were thrown into the water then, when a tuna pack appeared in the bait trail, a fish would be attached to the hook and dropped down to the feeding tuna.

This technique can still be used occasionally in sections of the North Sea, particularly in areas off the Norwegian coastline where blue fin still appear during the summer months.

In the warmer waters of the Atlantic – off Portugal, Madeira, the Canary Islands and the Azores – a similar method, using live rather than dead fish, can be highly effective. I once took fifty-three tuna in a three week period off Fayal in the Azores, all caught on live horse mackerel. The drawback to this technique is that it also attracts sharks: but if the angler is prepared to lose the odd set of terminal tackle to a big shark then the 'natural fish method' is one of the best ways of taking tuna.

Trolling has many advantages when compared with drift fishing. For a start, the baits are shown over a much wider area, and the cockpit of the boat does not become fouled by refuse from the natural baits. The only disadvantage is that the boat's engines are run continuously, making trolling a noisy way of spending a full day on the ocean.

Trolling for tuna usually consists of four baits (see Fig. 20) set at varying distances behind the boat. The two outside baits are fished off outriggers, while the two middle baits are fished on the flat line system, i.e. from rods set in special holders, usually situated on either side of the fighting chair. If the fish being hunted are on the shy side then most strikes will register on the long-range baits trolled from the outriggers. However, if the fish really go on the rampage then they will hit each and every bait in the water. On many occasions I have seen all four lures taken simultaneously. On one occasion, I saw all fish boated, but this is very unusual. A total 'hook up' usually ends with most, if not all, the lines being broken during the opening stages of the battle.

On a perfect day when tuna packs are sighted working shoals of bait fish, the baits can be trolled round or even through the centre of activity. On most days, however, the fish stay lower down in the water and then 'blind trolling' is the accepted method. On this sort of day, strikes usually occur once everybody on the boat has succumbed to the sunshine and steady beat of engines. The sudden snap of the outrigger clip or the high-pitched scream of a big reel being the first indication of a bite. Trolling in whichever style, is an exciting,

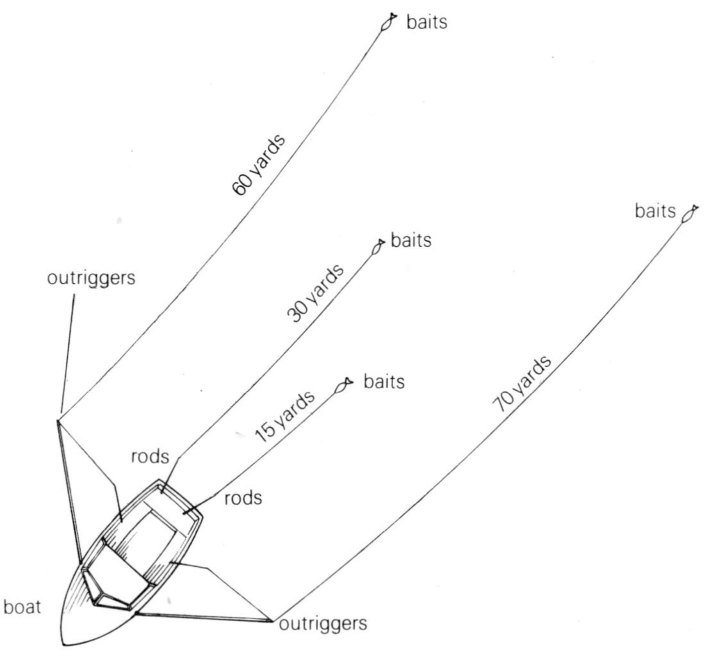

FIGURE 20   Trolling for tuna calls for four baits set at varying distances behind the boat.

totally fascinating and often highly productive style of big game fishing, never more so than on a day I had fishing for tuna off Madeira.

The day was flat calm, with not even the slightest breeze to disturb the oily sea. Apart from an occasional, isolated flying fish the surface of the Atlantic looked dead. Then, abruptly, everything changed as an immense shoal of big eyed tuna tore into a heavy pack of mackerel. Most of this activity lay dead ahead of our boat but breakaway packs of tuna were showing on all sides.

With the engines running flat out, and with the artificial lures skipping through our wake, we headed straight for the main centre of activity. As we neared the main feeding area we could see the explosions caused by striking tuna and the glint of thousands of airborne bait fish as they tried to escape from their giant predators.

Inshore from us the Island of Madeira was illuminated by sunlight so bright and clear that even at that distance tiny details of the white houses could be picked out. Under normal circumstances, the sheer beauty of the sunlit mountain would have held everyone's attention. But now, with the sea boiling with feeding fish, no one aboard our fishing boat paid the slightest attention to this incredible sight.

When the first strike came, and the big reel began to scream, all of the waiting and the long endless hours of trolling were forgotten. As always, the fish hooked itself and, as always, it followed the traditional fighting pattern of tuna, diving immediately straight down to the hoped for safety of dark water. At this stage I could do nothing but climb into the fighting chair and set the rod butt into the gimpole.

Any attempt to stop the first downward lunge of a big tuna is always an instant recipe for disaster. The trick is to let the fish run, and pray that it slows down before it takes every yard of line from your reel. Big eye tuna may not grow to the size of the giant blue fin tuna, but what they lack in size they certainly make up for in speed and determination.

This fish was no exception. It took a little over 300 yards of my line before slowing down, and even then it took nearly 50 more before finally coming to rest. The side plates of the Penn 12-0 reel were almost too hot to touch and as I started to increase the drag I knew I was in for a long hard slog before the fish would be back at gaffing level.

When a big tuna sounds in this manner its sheer bulk and broad, deep body act as a drogue. This fish was typical of all tuna, for after its first headlong plunge it levelled off, turned on its broad side and used the tremendous pressure of water to maintain its position.

For a while I was unable to gain line, but I knew that constant rod pressure would eventually begin to wear down the fish. Once I could get the fish to move I would be in a position to gain line, gradually working the fish back to surface level. The rod tip suddenly lifted, and I knew I had my fish on the move. At first I was only able to gain inches of line, but within minutes the inches had turned into yards as the fish started to swim upwards. By now the big reel was filling rapidly as I cranked its handle to gain more line. My main fear was that the fish would turn back down again for another run. Tuna usually fight in predictable style, and this includes at least two tremendous rushes for deep water. So the trick is to anticipate each rush, slackening the reel drag slightly to avoid the line parting under a sudden strain.

The fish came up at high speed, hit surface in a spectacular boil of white water and then plunged straight back down in top gear. This time the tuna did not win as much line and levelled off at a depth of about 100 yards, once again using its broad sides to hold its position through sheer strength and water pressure.

The moment it stopped its run, I began to pile on pressure. To give any tuna resting time is always a bad mistake and I had no intention of giving this fish time to regain its strength. Fortunately for me, the tuna did not maintain its position for long, and within two minutes of stopping it was on the move again, circling warily round the stern of the boat.

Applying maximum rod pressure I was able to gain line, gradually easing the fish upward a few inches at a time. With the reel spool almost re-filled I told the boat crew to put on their work gloves, ready to 'wire' the fish the moment the trace broke surface. When the fish came up it was obviously finished, and allowed itself to be pulled alongside and gaffed without putting up more than a feeble resistance. Later it weighed in at 256 pounds: not a monster and certainly not a record breaker, but a nice example of a big eye tuna.

Not all battles end this way. I remember on one occasion while fishing off Madeira that a big fish hit a trolled lure, hooked itself on impact and then went down deep and fast in typical tuna fashion. Everything about the strike and the diving run screamed tuna, yet half an hour later when I brought the fish to the surface I found myself apparently hooked to a huge shark.

This fish was not just big, it was enormous. On top of that it was obviously very active and angry. The second it surfaced it lashed the water to foam with its great tail, then dived again to a depth of over 100 fathoms. This time it did not fight tuna style, instead it raced round in jagging circles. Again I managed to bring it to the surface and again we had a good sighting of a very angry giant shark. On its third dive I applied maximum pressure in a vain attempt to slow things down and this time the corks on the rod handle began to buckle and split as the rod over flexed. At this stage I was convinced that the shark was foulhooked, and if that was the case I wanted to break off as fast as possible. Besides being no fun to play, a foulhooked fish is never eligible for a record, and if any fish was a record breaker then this one was.

By now the distorted rod corks had started to cut into my hands causing blisters which rapidly burst exposing raw flesh to the rough-edged corks, and at this stage the battle became painfully unpleasant. (Later I found pools of blood on either side of the fighting chair, and my hands had to remain bandaged for over three weeks.)

Again and again I brought the fish to the surface only to see it crash dive back into the depths. The fight was now becoming personal. I wanted to catch that fish more than any of the others I had ever hooked. I was well into the second hour of the fight and I began to cram on the power to finish the battle as quickly as possible. Luckily for me the fish appeared to be weakening. Twice more it was in sight, and then I got it up to the surface where it went totally wild.

Within seconds the great tail had thrashed the sea to foam, soaking both myself and the crew to the skin. The mate, however, had the trace in his hands and as he drew the fish closer the skipper quickly prepared to gaff the great fish. As soon as the gaff sank home the skipper leaned back to manhandle the giant fish alongside. Throughout all this the shark was frantically rolling and plunging and it rapidly became apparent to everyone that whatever the skipper had on his gaff it was not the shark. All hand were now busily helping to drag the fish from the sea and to our total surprise, our combined efforts produced not a shark but a beautiful big eye tuna.

To the second that the tuna dropped inboard the furious shark kept trying to eat it, and all became apparent. The shark had obviously sighted the hooked tuna seconds after the tuna had taken the bait. From that time on, the shark had kept after the hooked fish, obviously frightening the tuna so much that it had fought on in a totally un-tuna like manner. Every time I had pumped the tuna to the surface the giant shark had rushed in to attack, giving us the impression that it was firmly hooked. Once the tuna was safely aboard the shark vanished, obviously disappointed at losing a promising meal. The tuna weighed in at over 200 pounds, a nice but not outstanding fish, but one that I shall always remember.

Every big game angler has a wealth of anecdotes, and each has his favourite lost fish story. Mine concerns a giant blue fin tuna. Again this fish was hooked off Madeira, perhaps the best place in Europe to catch good tuna. Unfortunately it was hooked on borrowed tackle. The rod I was using was an old Hardy tuna rod, matched to a 16-0 reel of American origin.

The day had started well for me and I already had one nice big eye tuna aboard. The next strike came at midday, when a huge fish chopped a black-feather jig trolled directly behind the boat. I had a clear sighting of the fish as it nailed the jig and knew then that it was a monster. My estimate was between 800 and 1,000 pounds. Once again, typical of all tuna it dived straight down as it felt the hook. Giant tuna normally level off at about 300 or 400 yards but this fish just kept on going. With the boat's mate pouring water over the now-smoking reel I watched in disbelief as the line was stripped from the reel spool. In all I had already lost an incredible 1,000 yards of heavy dacron and, like it or not, I was convinced that the fish would carry on downwards until I finally ran out of line, at which stage a break would be inevitable.

Amazingly the fish stopped with only four turns of line left on the spool of the reel. A 16-0 reel is a huge, tough piece of machinery and to see the great spool virtually emptied was unnerving and almost unbelievable.

Fortunately for me the fish then began to move slowly upward, allowing me to regain my line fairly quickly. I knew that the fish was huge, and my intention was to try to finish this fight as quickly as possible. A great blue fin hooked over deep water can, and will, often fight on for hours. My best hope was to attempt to lead this one to the gaff before it really woke up. Initially the battle went my way. The fish came up steadily, allowing me to gain line. Then, with only an estimated 100 yards of line to regain, the fish went berserk.

It headed straight for the bottom in a staggeringly-powerful dive and in seconds I lost most of the regained line. The end plates of the big reel were now too hot to touch and once again it was necessary to pour water over the reel to cool it down. With over 600 yards of line ripped from the reel the tuna stopped and began to bang the trace with its vast tail. I knew then that I was in for the long and brutal battle I had hoped to avoid.

Wind and pump, pump and wind – the old, old routine of fighting a big fish – went on as the minutes ticked away. For most of this time I was on the winning side and gaining line, but I was still conscious that the huge fish had reserves of strength that were as yet untapped.

I have seen a great many apparently played-out blue fin break free in a wild, last ditch show of defiance. This fish did just that. One second it was coming up, slowly but steadily, the next it turned and dived at such speed that the old rod smashed six inches below the tip rig. Even at this stage I still had a sporting chance, for with most of the rod still intact I was able to apply pressure to the running fish.

I was so sure in my own mind that the fish was finished that I worked hard to get back the lost line. What I did not count on was the fish making a final dash for the depths and freedom: a dash that ripped all the rings from the rod. Obviously, I was out of the fight for it is impossible to play a big fish on just a reel alone, but at this stage the crew started to handline, in an attempt to save as much line as possible. The fish came up, breaking surface several yards from the boat.

Exhausted, the tuna lay motionless just opening and closing its mighty gill plates: the hook in plain view, hanging from a shred of skin. At the first renewed strain on the line, the hook fell clear and we watched as the giant fish slowly began to revive. Soon its tail began to work and within seconds it was drifting downwards out of sight.

The smashed and distorted rod is now on permanent exhibition in the Tourist Offices in Fayal, a reminder of a three and a half hour struggle with one of the ocean's giants.

Wreck Fishing

Wreck fishing provides anglers with the opportunity to catch specimen fish in large numbers. Unfortunately, most inshore wrecks in British and European waters have now been drastically overfished, by both rod and line anglers, and by commercial fishermen. This means that the top catches are now found on wrecks lying more than 20 miles out, a distance which can only be achieved in good weather conditions by large, fully-equipped licensed charter boats.

Accurate wreck location is essential. A few of the inshore wrecks can be lined up by shore marks, but under most circumstances wrecks nowadays are pinpointed by sophisticated electronic devices. The Decca Navigator is the best known example. The Navigator receives a continuous stream of signals from shore stations. These are displayed as numbers on green, red and purple dials which give an accurate crossbearing of the boat's position in relation to 'lanes' on a Decca chart, which lists the hundreds of wrecks plotted by hydrographic surveys.

Each wreck has its own set of co-ordinates, and when these are known it is possible to position a fishing boat right over the site. All wreck skippers keep a record of the crossbearing numbers. However, each year new wrecks are located and as each is likely to provide hot-fishing, at least at the beginning, most skippers try to keep newly discovered wrecks a personal secret. Some skippers go to great lengths to preserve their secret, only working a new hulk when no other vessel is in sight. This is understandable, for a skipper's reputation is based on the catches he can produce for his charter fishermen.

Should a competitor be sighted, the wreck is quickly abandoned to be fished on a future expedition!

Locating a wreck is one thing, anchoring on it is another and much less simple. Many wreck skippers have brought anchoring to a fine science and before letting go of their anchor are able to assess accurately the direction of tide, wind strength and how the wreck is lying in relation to prevailing conditions. Sometimes the anchor will be dropped several hundred yards uptide of the wreck, but by the time the warp has taken up the boat has drifted close enough to the required site for anglers to drop baits right back into the wreck, where the fish are most likely to congregate.

Many different species are found on wrecks but the sport is dominated by only a few: these are conger, cod, ling, pollack, coalfish and bream. The heavyweights like conger, cod and ling are taken on heavy duty tackle and big baits ledgered on the bottom. Pollack and coalfish fall to medium weight gear, on artificial and natural baits, fished between the wreckage and the surface, although it is generally the bottom 15 fathoms (90 feet) that is the productive zone. Black and red bream are caught by using more sensitive tackle fished right into the wreck.

Heavy Weight Tackle

Conger and ling reach enormous weights and over the past fifteen years records have increased regularly. The record conger is now a giant of 109 pound 6 ounces, caught by Robin Potter from Bristol who was fishing 22 miles south of Plymouth, on a wreck mark south-east of the Eddystone Lighthouse. Britain's biggest rod caught ling fell to Henry Solomons of Brixham, and was caught south of Dodman Point in Cornwall. This fish weighed 57 pound 2 ounces.

It is obvious that robust tackle is essential to deal successfully with such huge fish. The perfect combination for this heavyweight wrecking is a 50 pound test rod, with a 6/0 multiplier. The best reels are the Penn 6-0 or one of the British-made Tatler range. Both stand up to the brutal job of dragging endless great fish out of deep water. There are many

excellent rods available for wreck fishing and it pays to
purchase the best that you can afford. Terminal tackle for
bottom-dwelling fish should comprise a ledger rig of good
quality wire, 12 to 18 inches long, ending in a size 8-0 or 10-0
hook, preferably of the offset forged-eye type. A 3-0 swivel is
used to connect this to the reel line, and also stops the sliding
lead from running down to the hook. It is good practice to use
a 'rotten bottom' to hold the lead. This 'rotten bottom' (see
Fig. 21) is made from a short length of old line of lesser
breaking strain than the reel line, so that the old line will break
easily if the lead fouls up, leaving the trace, etc, intact.

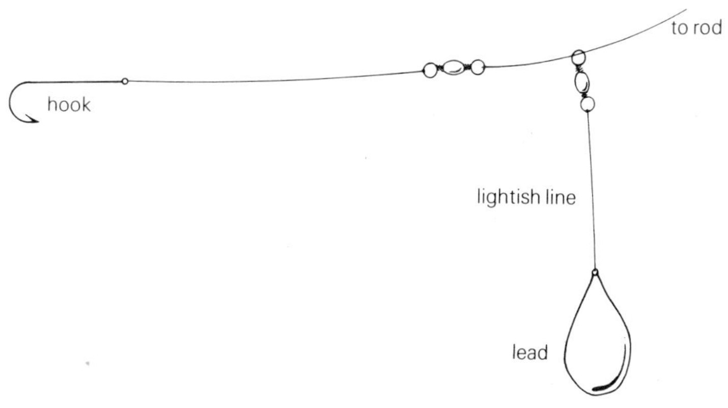

FIGURE 21 'Rotten bottom' tackle. If the lead fouls on the bottom then it
snaps off, leaving the hook and trace intact.

Choice of bait is up to you. All fish will, if truly hungry, take
a stale bait but it is my experience that a fresh bait always
produces most bites. All fish bite in different ways. A ling, for
example, is a greedy, aggressive feeder with a corresponding
bite. A conger, however, can be quite gentle, in spite of its
size, strength and reputation. As a big eel often mouths the
bait for some time, before actually sucking it in, only long
experience will tell you when to strike. The password to
success is *patience,* never be in a hurry.
When the rod tip indicates a bite, slack line should be

wound in slowly until full contact is made with the fish. Once hooked, the conger should immediately be levered into 'clear' water above the wreckage. Never give line. Take the risk of being broken, but get the fish up and away from the wreck. Line can be given later, under pressure through the reel clutch. Big conger – those weighing more than 50 pounds – will make many dives in their attempts to regain the sanctuary of the wreck, and huge eels of 80 or 100 pounds have been known to dive successfully back from the surface, through 50 or so fathoms, and lose themselves safely in the jumble of wreckage.

Congers should always be brought to the gaff in an exhausted condition. A 'green' fish can be difficult to gaff and decidedly dangerous once gaffed.

Ling and conger take the bait in different ways. The moment a ling bite is felt, the hook can be struck home and the fish dragged up and away from the bottom. Ling weighing 30 pounds plus give a good account of themselves, and experienced wreck anglers can easily tell the difference in take between conger and ling, and react accordingly.

Big cod are less easy to catch. These fish seldom bite in a set fashion. Oddly enough most wrecks have a resident shoal of hefty cod. Very occasionally these go on a wild feeding spree. I was on a trip once off the Isle of Wight when no less than fifty 20 pound plus cod were boated.

Medium Weight Tackle

Wreck fishing for pollack and coalfish provides great sport. Both species are good fighters, and the line-stripping plunge of even a 15 pound coalfish is one of the most thrilling experiences in sea fishing. During the summer months most are caught on medium weight tackle from anchored boats. The usual rig for this is a single hook, size 4/0 attached to an 18 foot trace, worked from an 8 inch boom. The boom keeps the trace from tangling with the reel line as the bait plummets to the bottom. The bait or lure is then retrieved steadily until a fish strikes. Once hooked, the fish will make a characteristic plunge, and line must be given or a break is certain. The coalfish is a better fighter than pollack, because it is less affected by the alteration of water pressure caused by changes in depth. An average 15 pound specimen will make at least half a dozen good, fast runs before reaching the surface. Pollack, on the other hand, are easily weakened by changing water pressure and when pumped up too quickly arrive lifeless at the surface.

The top time off the coast of Europe for both species is between November and March, when females are heavy with roe. So many fish congregate in this season over deep-water wrecks that echo sounders and fish finders sometimes record what appears to be a solid mass of fish above the wreck.

Winter Wreck Fishing

Most winter wreck fishing is done on the drift. For several reasons the best catches are made during spring tides, when the fast run of water stirs the fish into a bout of frenzied feeding. Once in a feeding mood, the fish strike fiercely at both natural baits and lures without hesitation. Big tides also ensure fast drifts across the wreckage, which make it possible for anglers to get in as many as 30 or 35 drifts during a single tide.

Drift fishing is always most successful when anglers work from one side only of the boat. Because a charter boat moves sideways, down the length or across the hulk, the lines stream out naturally from one side only. Working from the wrong side, the lines go under the keel, which makes it almost impossible to remain in direct contact with the bait or with a hooked fish. These lines also often tangle with those streaming away correctly, causing a severe waste of valuable fishing time.

Most winter fishing is done with heavy-weight nylon paternosters, rigged with artificial eels on short snoods. For a two hook rig the nylon must not be less than 50 pounds breaking strain, and if three artificials are being used (which I do not advise) the line strength must be stepped up to a breaking strain of 80 pounds. Even this line can be snapped like cotton as two big fish head in opposite directions after taking the lures simultaneously. There is not a great deal of skill in this style of fishing, but it can be great fun. The lures, weighted with at least a pound of lead, are allowed to plummet at high speed to the bottom. They are often taken on the drop, by fish cruising as much as ten fathoms (60 feet) above the wreckage. The second this happens, the multiplier reel should be put into gear, so that the full weight of two or even three specimen-size fish come on to the rod. The resulting jerk will usually set the hooks solidly home.

Successful winter wrecking on the drift depends greatly on the skill of the skipper, who must set up each drift to take full advantage of the wreck's position and who should know exactly where the high sections of the wreck are situated. As he watches the sounder, a stream of instructions will be shouted back to the anglers from the wheelhouse. 'Up 60 foot', or 'We're over, drop back 30 foot', and so on. Even with the shouted warnings, a lot of expensive tackle will be lost and winter wrecking can be an expensive business.

Large *pirks* or *jiggers* produce excellent catches. These pirks can be bought, or else made up from chrome tube filled with lead. Shop-bought pirks are sold complete with a giant treble hook. Such hooks have a tendency to foulhook many fish – hence the name 'ripper', which is often applied to such rigs. No true angler likes to foulhook fish, and most people change the treble hook for a 10-0 single.

When cod are on the move, I like to use a wire trace of 8 inches length between the pirk and hook (see Fig. 22). The hook is then baited with either mackerel or squid. This rig also works well for ling.

A great deal of strength is required to work a big pirk correctly for long periods. The results, however, are often worth the effort. I have taken cod to 35 pounds on baited pirks and ling to a fraction over 40 pounds. Many anglers cannot stand the constant effort of continuously working a pirk, but those who can often become the top scorers on the boat. It is the next day however, that the price is paid, when all the aches and pains set in in earnest!

Light Weight Tackle

To get a little light relief it is sometimes nice to try for the flyweights of wreck fishing – the sea bream. Black bream are

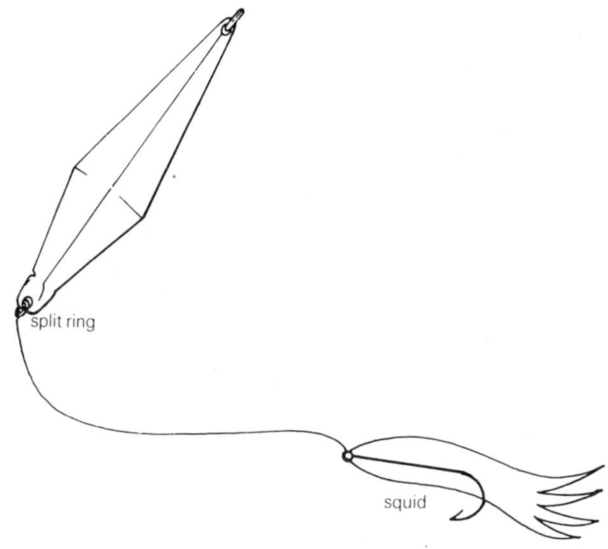

FIGURE 22   A pirk with 8 inch wire trace between its split ring and the hook, which is baited with squid or mackerel. This is lethal for good-sized cod or ling.

usually summer visitors only to a wreck, but red bream appear to be permanent residents.

To get the best from bream fishing the most-useful rig (even for deep-water sport) is a spinning rod with a length of 8 or 9 feet, matched with a light multiplier.

End tackle should be a two-hook paternoster with 9 inch snoods made up from monofilament line of 20 pound breaking strain and I/O forged hooks.

Squid provides the best bream bait. It cuts well into thin strips and is tough enough to stay on the hook. Although several bream can be caught on the same bait I prefer to change baits each time a fish is boated. Sea bream bite sharply, and so should be struck very quickly. Both species make first-class table fish, although I prefer eating red bream to black.

Coalfish

Pound for pound the coalfish is probably the finest fighting species found around a wreck. Similar in appearance to pollack, the coalfish has a more muscular body which gives it a faster turn of speed than pollack of similar size.

When hooked, a large coalfish will normally dive for the security of the wreck. To get the most out of catching coalfish it is best to use 20 or 30 pound IGFA rated tackle. The 20 pound gear is the nicest to use but most charter skippers insist on their anglers using 30 pound class tackle. Fortunately, having many friends who own and skipper wreck fishing boats, I have been able to join private 'fun' trips where 20 pound class tackle has been allowed.

Large coalfish are commonest in the winter months and I recall one trip from Fowey in Cornwall when – despite the forecast of increasing winds – we resolutely set off to fish the distant wreck of a wartime liberty ship.

The wreck took a little over four hours to reach and by the time we arrived the wind had risen considerably, making it obvious that – at best – we would only be able to fish for a short while.

It was known that the wreck held a number of large coalfish and with these in mind I set up a single flying boom to which I attached a twelve foot trace. My lure was a single fluorescent yellow 'red-gill' sand eel. The skipper was not at all happy with my choice of bait colour, preferring black or red eels. However, as the yellow had caught me many good fish on previous trips, I stuck to my guns and gave it a try. The day was hardly pleasant. The sky was dark and the sea lumpy but even so, it was good to be fishing if only for a short period.

In those days – and this was a few years ago – the technique was to drop the terminal tackle down until the lead hit the wreck. As soon as contact was made, the reel was pushed into gear and the reel handle cranked as fast as possible. Fifty high speed revolutions were the norm and if a fish did not take the lure during that period the tackle was lowered again and the process repeated until a fish struck the racing red-gill. Bites on this method were invariably savage: one second the eel would be rising at high speed, the next the rod would be practically wrenched from your hands.

On this day, fish were on the move from the outset. I took a nice 20 pound cod on my first drop, on the next, a pollack of around 15 pounds weight. Then the skipper hooked and boated a smallish coalfish weighing an estimated 14 pound. The fast-winding technique takes plenty of getting used to, but once a routine has been established it can be a pleasant method to use. To make things easier, I was using a special Penn 6-0 reel fitted with a high speed gear combination. This reel is perfectly adapted for the sort of fishing described, and takes much of the strain off an angler's winding arm and shoulder.

After that first coalfish two drifts passed without a sniff of a fish. On the next drift, however, I had just about reached the limit of 50 turns when I hit something like a brick wall. A fraction of a second later the wall turned into a mid-Channel Inter-City Express, ripping line off my reel at high speed as it headed for the wreck and safety. There was little doubt of its identity, only a big coalfish could strike and run like that.

At this stage of my fishing career I had yet to take a coalfish of more than 20 pounds in weight. I had taken many coalies up to 19 pounds, but that 20 pound target had always managed to elude me. I instinctively knew that this battling fish was the one I wanted. Wreck fishing is a brutal sport: give line too easily and the fish will smash the line in the wreck, use too much force and the line will snap under the strain. Luck as well as skill plays an important part in wreck fishing, and I hoped on this day that luck was on my side.

At first the coalfish had everything its own way. My advantage, however, was that the fish had struck the lure at the tail end of the drift. This meant that it had been hooked clear of the wreck and would have to take a great deal of line to regain its sunken fortress.

Despite my advantage the fish took a great deal of line at great speed and was stopped with only yards to go to achieve its objective. A hooked coalfish may make a number of dives for freedom, but its first run is always the most significant. If this can be stopped the fish loses a little of its fire and once this has happened, if the angler keeps the fish on the move under constant rod pressure, it will finally begin to spiral up towards the surface.

Unlike cod and ling, which 'blow out' due to pressure change, coalfish normally arrive on the surface in perfect condition. More than one large coalfish has broken free within inches of the gaff, and it pays to pay constant attention to the reel drag until the fish is safely inboard.

Knowing that the fish was now in open water I settled down to enjoy the battle. Under such circumstances a rod in the 20 pound class is a joy to use. Strong enough to apply pressure yet light enough to give maximum sport, such a rod can be made to do wonders.

I did not keep track of the time I spent playing the coalfish, but I estimate that over ten minutes passed before the fish began grudgingly to give ground. Slowly but surely the line began to build up on the reel, until finally deep below the boat we could see the fish coming up. The second it hit surface I knew I had broken my coveted 20 pound barrier, hopefully by several pounds.

In peak condition, the fish stood out in stark relief to the dark blue sea. Down its side ran a distinctive white lateral stripe, which seemed to glow, while in the corner of its neat mouth I could clearly see the projecting head of my fluorescent yellow sand eel. Once inboard, the fish was weighed in at a fraction over 24 pounds: a fine specimen and a personal best of species for me. A best which I have yet to beat.

One day I hope to catch a larger specimen, for coalfish certainly attain weights in excess of 35 pounds and fish of close to 40 pounds have been caught by commercial methods, while most experienced wreck anglers have hooked huge coalfish only to lose them on that first hard, long run for freedom. Indeed, I lost such a specimen less than three days after catching my 24 pounder.

We were out fishing a new wreck which was thought to hold big cod. I had already caught some fine cod on a large pirk bait when the lure was hit at high speed by a fish which promptly crash-dived straight into the wreck. I was using a 50 pound class outfit, which should have been heavy enough to have stopped any coalfish that ever lived. This fish, however, continued to take line against maximum rod pressure and within seconds of hooking up I was left to wind in a loose and chafed line.

There could be no question of the fish's identity. Only a coalfish or a shark could produce such speed and a shark would not have dived into the wreck for safety. Obviously I did not see this fish, but I am quite convinced that it was a

monster coalfish. I can only hope that it managed to shake off
my lure from its mouth and regain its freedom.

Cod and Ling

Although very different in outward appearance, cod and ling
share similar feeding habits. Both species shoal in loose
formation and both have a tendency to swim just above a
wreck but below the pollack and coalfish shoals. Many get
caught on red-gill or 'edystone' eels but for consistent results
I find it pays to fish a lure and natural bait combination.

Of the two species ling are the most voracious but, on a
good day when the fish are well on feed, cod will snatch at
every bait they see. Although these days are rare they do
occur, and when they do some marathon catches can result.

When wreck fishing for cod and ling I invariably use a 50
pound class rod; a Tatler IV or V reel; and line of 50 pound
breaking strain. I prefer to use dacron line rather than nylon as
dacron is thinner in diameter. As far as terminal tackle is
concerned I shun the use of multi-hook rigs, preferring to stick
to a simpler basic rig that has instant appeal to the cod and ling
packs. My choice of terminal rig is dictated by the size of the
fish normally taken over the wrecks I fish.

Cod and ling of 20 plus pounds are the norm for wreck
fishing. Fish of over 30 pounds are a regular occurrence and
40 or even 50 pound fish could appear at any time. My
favourite wreck-fishing grounds in British waters are a rich
area stretching from the Isle of Wight down the coast to
Cornwall. Further north, however, where fish tend to decrease
in size, two hook or three hook rigs are perfectly acceptable but
in the south, three large fish hooked simultaneously soon lead
to smashed tackle.

For this South Coast fishing I use a large chromed pirk-type
lure, to which I attach an 8 or 9 inch trace made up from
nylon-covered wire of 100 pound breaking strain. To the end
of this trace I attach a 10-0 flat forged, and carefully
sharpened, hook. This hook is then baited with a fillet of fish or
a piece of squid or cuttlefish (see Fig. 22). The pirk is then
attached to the reel line with a 5 foot length of 80 pound
breaking strain nylon. This heavy nylon acts as a buffer to

both the fish and any accidental chafing that occurs when the pirk drops or scrapes over or into the actual superstructure of the wreck.

This set up is tough tackle designed to catch big fish; if, on the other hand, I was to go wreck fishing off Scotland or the north-east coast I would leave my pirk type baits at home and make up a three hook terminal rig, incorporating three brightly coloured plastic squid known generally as 'muppets' (see Fig. 23). These baits are fished above a lead and worked by raising and lowering the rod tip. This type of terminal rig

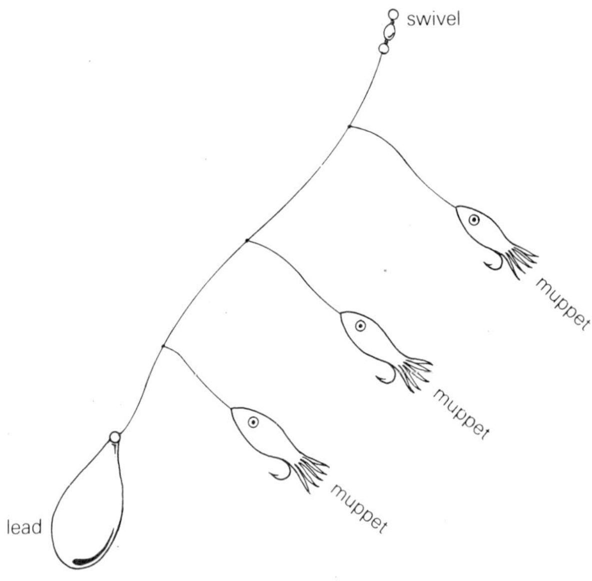

FIGURE 23   A 'muppet' rig made up of three plastic squid fished above a lead. This is a deadly set up for small cod or coalfish.

can be extremely deadly for small cod, pollack and coalfish. The trick to wreck fishing is to keep the end tackle as simple as possible.

Tackle losses are an integral part of wreck fishing and to cut costs pirk baits can be made up at home, using lead-filled sections of chrome piping to form the body of the pirk. The end of the pipe can then be hammered flat and slightly offset to give the bait additional movement. These home-made pirk baits catch as many fish as their expensive shop-bought counterparts, and save the angler many pounds during the course of an average season.

One of the best-ever days I had wreck fishing for cod was off the south coast of England over a wreck known locally as 'Daddy Long Legs'.

The wreck was a big one, and the original explosion which sent her down to the sea bed must have been enormous. No one seems to know the full story or the ship's name. Simply that she and her crew fell victim to a lurking U Boat during the last war. Sited some 35 miles from the Isle of Wight, she sank in nearly 50 fathoms (300 feet) of water with many of her crew probably still aboard.

She had been fished twice only to our knowledge, and on our visit she had not been tapped for over twelve months. The two earlier wrecking trips had produced the usual mixed bag of cod, pollack, ling and the odd red bream. My main interest was the cod and ling, although I intended to spend the final half-hour on the red bream.

The diminutive red bream is the most succulent of all wreck fish, particularly when cooked on a barbecue. And with food in mind I had every intention of trying to put a good bag of bream on the boat, but only after I had filled a few boxes with cod and ling.

On this day I had brought along a 50 pound outfit, and a lighter 20 pound rod for bream fishing. Bait, as always, was a combination of large pirk and natural, in this instance long slices of cuttlefish. For deep water fishing, where visibility is down to a minimum, the white flesh of a cuttlefish or squid catches more fish than the more conventional and darker mackerel fillet. Probably because the white flesh of the cuttle or squid shows up well in the dark water and attracts hunting fish by sight as well as smell.

On the first drift over the wreck I dropped the heavy baited pirk down fast, until I felt it bump bottom. Instantly the rod arched over as a large fish struck at the bait and solidly hooked itself. From the style of bite I was certain it was a cod and a good one. Minutes later I was proved right as a large cod spiralled up through the clear blue water.

Practically every angler on the boat was into a fish and it was obvious that we had started fishing at exactly the right state of the tide. On the next drop down, the line slackened abruptly long before my bait reached wreck level. I knew with certainty that a ling was responsible. These huge eel-like fish are past masters at intercepting a bait, and as I struck I felt the familiar surge as the ling turned and headed for cover.

All large ling fight well at first but unfortunately they are extremely susceptible to pressure change, and once they reach mid water their swim bladders fill with air and they cease to fight, usually arriving on the surface more dead than alive. This is a shame, for in full fighting trim ling are capable of providing some great sport.

By this stage both skipper and crew were busy gaffing a seemingly endless stream of big fish. Many of the fish being brought inboard were cod: big hefty fish weighing on average between 20 and 30 pounds. One fish boated was so large that the skipper stopped gaffing to weigh it. Thirty six pounds was his verdict, a big fish by anyone's standards and we all hoped it was an omen of the sport ahead of us for conditions were as near perfect as they can get. A flat oily sea, bright sun and endless visibility.

Visibility is a great advantage when fishing mid-Channel wreck marks. Few people have any idea how much shipping uses the Channel each day of the year. And there is nothing worse than fishing a wreck in poor visibility, when you can hear an endless procession of huge engines but cannot see the passing ships. On this day we hardly had time to look for shipping. Each drift produced instant action.

To get down to sea bed level as quickly as possible, I changed to a huge pirk weighing 24 ounces. This monster lure was heavy enough to go straight through the waiting ling pack, down to where the big cod lurk. However, my lure fouled the wreck on its first drop down and there it stayed. Fortunately, it takes only seconds to knot on a large pirk and I lost only a short spell of precious fishing time.

This time my tackle bumped just once, and then the rod slammed down hard as a big fish engulfed the trailing bait. Lifting my rod tip to set the hook, I felt the fish begin to roll over in typical big cod style. A large cod tends to roll and shake its head in an attempt to throw the hook. This trait is useful to the wreck angler, for it allows a few moments grace to pump the fish up and away from the wreckage. Taking full advantage of the situation I piled on pressure, cranking the reel handle as fast as possible to gain precious line before the fish realised it was in mortal danger. Like many big cod this one was slow on the uptake, and I had it up a good 50 feet or more before it changed tactics and attempted to crash dive for the sea bed.

With my heavy rod bent into full battle curve and the clutch of my big Tatler giving line grudgingly, I knew I was in a position to dominate the battle. Big cod fight all the way and this one was no exception. Twice it was above the mid-water mark and twice it turned and headed back for the wreck. I admired its tenacity but knew barring accidents that the fish was mine. Sure enough, it soon came into sight. A huge pale shape, rising rapidly until its yellow-gold flanks broke surface.

The most impressive thing about a big cod is its huge head and vast, gaping mouth. This one had a mouth like a bucket and a huge pot belly, a sure sign of a big cod in first class condition. The skipper, aware of its size and not wishing it to lose weight, gaffed it neatly through the side of the jaw, boated it and in seconds it was being weighed. On first sight I had been certain it would weigh in at more than 40 pounds, but I was wrong. The fish weighed 38½ pounds, and obviously I was a bit disappointed. My personal best for the species weighed 43 pounds and I had hoped to beat that weight. Despite this, it was a great fish and one I was happy to catch.

Over the next hour and a half the fish came thick and fast. Ten rods continually hauling out big fish can tot up a huge weight of prime fish and at the end of the session we had an estimated 4,000 pounds of big fish on the deck. With the exception of two comparatively small pollack, the catch was made up entirely of ling and cod. Ling were by far the predominant species but a head count showed 53 big cod in the boat as well as over 150 prime ling.

This figure was for whole fish. We also had an assortment of half ling and tailless cod, each the victim of a pair of huge sharks. These marauders had shown up half way through the session. One minute someone was pumping up a good fish, then the fish stopped fighting and lost most of its weight. When the puzzled angler finally wound in he had half a fish. In one case just the head of a ling was left, its body chopped cleanly off right behind the gills. For a long time the sharks stayed deep, hitting our hooked fish at the mid-water mark, but gradually growing bolder they finally cruised into sight some 40 to 50 feet beneath the boat.

To say they were big would be to do them an injustice: they were enormous. Both looked to be around 12 feet in length, and weight in excess of 500 pounds. Although they were clearly visible it was impossible to ascertain from our position whether they were porbeagle or mako shark. My belief was that they were mako. I have caught a great many huge mako, in various parts of the world and these fish moved in that easy, yet questioning way typical of a hunting mako.

Although we did not have any shark tackle aboard, one angler was using an 80 pound rod with line to match, so a wire trace was hastily improvised from a length of nylon-coated wire with a 50 pound breaking strain, to which a 10-0 hook was crimped. This hook was baited with a long flap of ling, fresh cut from the side of one of the mutilated fish. This was dumped straight down from the side of the boat and as it sank both shark cruised up towards it. There did not appear to be any difference in length or weight between the two fish. Both were obviously hungry and as the ling flap sank within reach, both fish rushed it.

Seconds later one shark was hooked and the big Tatler V reel began to scream and smoke as the shark tore off at least a 100 yards of line. The fish was fast and strong, and for three-quarters of an hour it stayed well away from the boat. Finally, with no sign of the shark weakening, the trace parted under pressure and the shark of a lifetime was gone.

On inspection, the nylon-covered trace was shown to have frayed in many places: further proof to me at least, that such wire is of little use when shark hunting. The angler was obviously disappointed but also relieved, the fight had been brutal and coming as it did – after several hours of intensive wreck fishing – the strain on his arms, legs and back muscles was nearly unbearable.

I too was most disappointed. Not because the shark had

broken free but because I had not had the opportunity to see it clearly and positively identify it to my own satisfaction. Argument raged on the four-hour steam back to port as to whether it was a porbeagle or mako, with most favouring the view that it was a 'beagle'. The main evidence offered for this being that the shark made no attempt to jump during the battle.

It is a popular and widely-held belief that all mako sharks leap repeatedly when hooked. This is far from true. I have caught many mako, but only a few displayed aerobatic tendencies, and nothing will ever convince me that the fish was a porbeagle. In my mind it is established as a mako and a big one at that, but the truth is that no one will ever know for sure which kind of shark it was that fought so long and hard over the torpedo-shattered remains of that unknown wreck.

Wrecking for Conger

Sunken wrecks off the coast of Britain and mainland Europe are famous for producing massive catches of huge conger. So much so, that most anglers now assume that if they want to catch a monster eel it is essential to go wreck fishing. Records show that this is far from true, for many huge eels have been taken or found in relatively shallow water.

Top of the list of those found must be a gigantic 180 pound specimen washed ashore on the French coast in 1961. Before this, a 142 pound eel was found on Walcott beach in Norfolk. In 1965, a 101 pounder was accidentally netted by a prawn trawler operating off Berwick. While pride of place of those caught must go to a 250 pound specimen taken by a Belgian trawler in 1962.

Numerous other specimens – between 80 and 100 pounds – have also been recorded from many other areas. From the weights quoted above it is obvious that eels *can* reach weights in excess of 200 pounds although eels of 100 pounds or more are still a rarity, mainly because such fish are rarely hooked far from cover and so have no trouble smashing tackle.

Wrecks must, however, still be regarded as the prime target for a dedicated conger enthusiast. A sunken and shattered wreck provides thousands of suitable places for conger to hole up, and this – coupled with the plentiful supply of food fish, such as pouting and red sea bream – ensures a substantial and readily available number of resident conger eels.

Conger eels are not a shoal fish. Each eel is a loner,

interested only in its own way of life. All the same, the average wreck can hold hundreds and possibly even thousands of good-sized conger eels.

The interesting thing is that most wreck eels weigh upwards of 30 pounds: small eels being noticeable by their absence. The reason for this is almost certainly the cannibalistic tendency of the larger fish. A 50 pound eel can easily hunt down and eat a 15 pounder, and any such fish that enters a wreck obviously has a short life expectancy.

Tackle

Conger are rough, tough individuals that show little regard for other life, and absolutely no respect for fishing tackle! Wreck fishing for conger is a rugged sport, which calls for brute force rather than refined technique, and this should be taken into account when selecting a set of tackle specifically for wreck fishing for conger.

Rods

Some very large eels have been taken on 50 and even 30 pound class outfits. Such fish, in my opinion, can only be regarded as lucky catches.

A light rod does not normally have the power necessary to 'skuldrag' a big eel out of a wreck, and it would seem that most of the large eels caught on lightish tackle are fish hooked away from the main body of a wreck.

Reels

Because of these factors the most practical outfit to employ is an 80 pound class rod, matched to a Tatler V or a Penn 6-0 reel, preferably fitted with a high-speed gear system which allows for rapid line recovery.

Lines

Whichever reel is chosen it should be filled to capacity with a nylon line of 80 pound breaking strain. This line should be wound on to the reel under heavy pressure.

If it is only loosely spooled the nylon line will contract in use and may shatter or warp the reel spool. Many huge conger have been lost when a spool has disintegrated under the strain of contracting nylon.

In an ideal world it would be preferable to use a dacron (polyester fibre) line which is stretch free, and therefore does not contract. Unfortunately dacron frays easily when scraped over a rough surface and as most conger are taken on baits dropped right into the wreck, dacron is simply not a practical proposition.

Traces

Although rod, line and reel take tremendous amount of abuse while wrecking for giant conger, it is the terminal tackle that is subjected to the most punishment. Luckily wreck conger are not subtle feeders; and this allows the angler to make and use traces that most other fish would shy away from. Refined trace material such as nylon-covered wire is of little use to the conger fisherman. In fact, many experienced anglers, make their traces out of fencing wire, and some monster eels have been caught on this type of trace.

The advantage of a fencing-wire trace is that it is cheap to make and, therefore, expendable. I have fished such traces on many occasions, but much prefer to make my own traces from stranded steering wire. This is available from most good chandler's shops. I make my steering wire traces up in 15 inch lengths from chandlers and the same chandlers will crimp a swivel on one end and a hook on the other.

In theory, it is easy to put on the crimps at home, but in practice I find it best to have the crimps put on professionally with a special crimping machine. Once crimped in this way, the crimps will never slip under pressure. When having crimps put on by a chandler, make sure that the chandler covers the loose end of the wire with the crimp (see Fig. 24). If a protruding end is left the wire will slowly splay out and may well slash someone's hand when they take hold of the trace to try to control a boated eel.

Hooks

Big baits appeal to big conger, which means hook sizes should

118

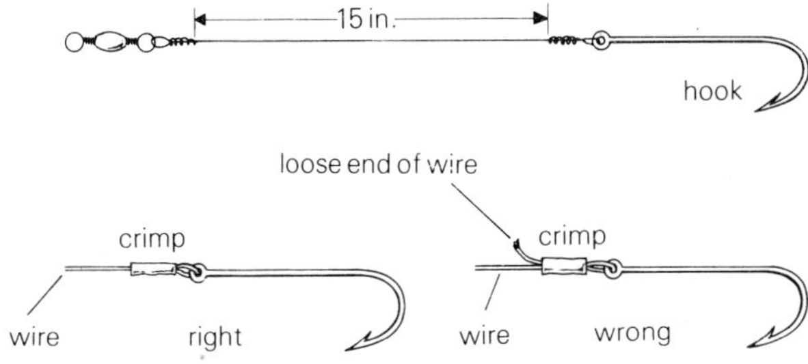

FIGURE 24   A good conger trace (*top*) can be made from 15 inches of 'steering wire' available from a chandler. To strengthen the trace (*bottom*) use crimps at both the hook and swivel end of the wire. These should be fitted professionally by the chandler. When having a crimp fitted make sure that it covers the loose end of the wire, otherwise the wire will fray and may inflict a nasty gash when someone is boating an eel.

also be large. I use 10-0 or 12-0 Mustad Seamaster hooks, honed to as sharp a point as possible.

Always remember that it is your hook that takes the strain. You may have the best rod and reel money can buy but it is your hook that links you to the fish. Mustad Seamaster hooks are not cheap but they are the best and I have never seen or heard of one parting under strain.

Swivels

Hooked conger often spin repeatedly round and round. These tactics put terrific additional strain on the terminal tackle. Because of this, I like to use large top-quality swivels for all my conger fishing. Probably the best swivel currently available is the Berkeley swivel in a 4-0 or 5-0 size. These swivels turn freely and are designed to withstand enormous pressures. Like the Mustad Seamaster hooks, I have yet to see one of these break down in use.

The quality factor cannot be too fully stressed. Conger are savage fish which have a style of fighting that rapidly shows up any weakness in tackle. The trick is to make sure that *all* your tackle is capable of withstanding the tremendous punishment handed out by a hooked and desperate eel.

Location and Methods

The wreck we were fishing dated back to the First World War and, as far as we could judge, it was still practically intact. On the screen of the echo sounder it looked high off the sea bed, like a huge upthrust finger.

Resting in nearly 60 fathoms (360 feet) of water it was not an easy mark to fish but with a fair tide and calm weather it was well worth a try, for it was known to hold a large number of good-sized conger eels, some of them well over 100 pounds in weight.

We had already fished the wreck twice before, taking huge catches of pollack, ling and cod in the process. Now we felt sure we had cleared away sufficient bottom fish to let us drop our baits right into the wreck where, we hoped, they would be found and taken by the resident eels.

It may sound strange to speak of 'clearing' a wreck before conger fishing but it has to be done, otherwise the free swimming species intercept the bait long before it reaches conger level. The catches so far had been vast and a look at the echo sounder showed only a slight smear on the screen, indicating that few fish remained hovering over the wreck. Two days previously a vast black cloud had hung there above the sunken ship.

Feeling confident of success, we waited patiently for the boat to take up a position from which we could drop our baits directly into the wreck. When the skipper gave us a thumbs up ten baits hit the water together and, as we 'thumbed' the reel spools so that the baits descended at an even speed, we all hoped that the day would produce a record conger eel.

Wreck eels often pounce on a bait the second it hits bottom, and this is exactly what happened in my case. I felt the big lead bump and as instantly felt the sullen dragging pull of a biting eel. There is no finesse about wreck fishing for conger. Give the fish but an inch of slack line and it will immediately back into its hole, wrap its strap-like tail round something solid and wait patiently for the angler to break his line, so the second I felt that eel on the bait I struck hard back and began to crank the handle of my big reel.

Fluster a conger and you can often lift it clear of the wreck before it can muster its wits or start battle. Quite obviously this one did not expect to be skuldragged up and out of the wreckage, and for a few vital seconds it allowed itself to be pulled upwards.

I suppose I gained about 20 yards of line before the fish woke up to its predicament. When it did realise the danger, however, it went totally berserk. Initially, it fought in the arm-jerking 'figure of eight' style used by all large conger. This allowed me to gain another few precious yards of line, before the fish turned in a great sweep, put its head down and crash dived towards the wreckage and safety.

My 80 pound class rod hooped-over into full battle curve, while the clutch of the big reel moaned and whirred as the frenzied eel took out line. But not even a big shark could have taken out more than ten yards of line against the sort of pressure I was applying and the conger was forced to change its tactics, allowing me to gain line rapidly as the fish swam upwards.

Reaching mid-water the eel then began to shake its head, jerking the rod tip round and down almost rhythmically. From this time onwards, the battle went all my way, with the eel coming up steadily until it hit surface and began to spin.

All down the side of our boat other anglers fought similar battles. Most brought their catch up to the gaff but two lost both their eels and terminal gear to the wreck.

With the boat crew busy gaffing, cutting off traces and dropping conger into the fish hold, the boat became a frantic hive of activity. New traces were knotted on, fresh baits cut and mounted on big hooks, and trace and bait dropped back down to the wreck. Nobody bothered to weigh or segregate the larger eels. The best of the fish we had in looked to be around 60 pounds in weight. A good sized conger but not in the class we had hoped for.

Still the wreck we were over was obviously fishing well and, sure enough, it was not long before the first really hefty eel was in the boat. This fish – weighing in at a fraction over 90 pounds – was a perfect example of an eel in peak condition. Short in length with a huge girth, it fought well and looked every ounce of its weight.

Naturally enough, this conger stirred everyone's imagination. After all a mark which could produce a 90 pounder could just as easily yield larger specimens, possibly well in excess of the 100 pound mark. By this stage we all had the measure of the wreck, and fish were coming aboard in rapid order.

It is easy to lose track of numbers caught under such circumstances but by counting made-up traces I could keep a tally of how many eels I had taken. I had started with 20 traces, lost one set of tackle in the wreck and had fourteen traces left, so my catch this far had been five eels, ranging from 30 pounds up to about 60 pounds in weight.

With my tackle back down in the wreckage I tightened up the line and, as I did so, the rod tip slammed hard down. This was by far the most violent bite of the day and its viciousness caught me by surprise. Despite this I still managed to strike and heave upwards, only to feel everything go solid. The eel had obviously managed to slither to safety under some wreckage and there it intended to stay.

When a large wreck eel does this, most anglers 'hardline' until their line parts under the strain. I will only break out in this fashion as a last resort, my standard tactic being to slacken the line and hope that the eel will assume it is now out of danger and can resume feeding. This may sound unlikely, but conger eels are tough creatures who think little of moving and feeding with a big hook and trace still attached to their iron jaw.

For several minutes nothing happened, then the line drew taut and I felt my rod tip begin to pull down as the fish moved off. This time I did not hesitate: I had that eel up and out of the wreck in seconds. It rose upward so easily that I thought for a few seconds it was a small one which had just struck hard when taking the bait. Realising its danger, however, the eel dived back for the sea bed with such power and speed that I knew for certain it was a monster.

As always, the spring of the big rod turned the fish with only yards to spare. Instantly the eel changed tactics, 'figure of eighting' at high speed in an attempt to break free. When this failed it began to twist: slowly at first, then at high speed causing the reel line to sing under the pressure and my rod tip to jerk and shudder alarmingly. This twisting action of a conger will often tear a hook free but in this instance it seemed I was lucky, and the hook appeared to hold fast.

It was not long before I had the fish coming up at a good speed. Twice it tried to dive, and twice the rod took the speed out of its rushing downwards plunge. Finally it was in sight, still swimming fairly strongly but obviously tiring. When it hit surface we could all see that it was the kind of conger every wreck angler dreams about. To say it was a monster would be a gross understatement. This eel was gigantic, huge. Even the skipper whistled when he saw its length and girth.

At first, on surfacing, it thrashed the water to foam but as it quietened down we could see the conger clearly, and just as clearly see that the hook was attached by only a tiny shred of white skin. Still more than one monster conger has been brought aboard safely, only to have the hook drop out at the last second. The skipper reached out to set the gaff and as he did so the fish spun once, wrapped the trace round the gaff and the hook tore free, allowing the vast eel to glide down out of our sight.

My estimate put that eel at 100 pounds plus. The skipper thought it would weigh a great deal more, exactly how much more he would not say at the time. Several years later he told me quietly that in his opinion that eel would have topped the 109½ pound conger record by a good ten pounds.

My disappointment at losing the eel was shared by everyone aboard. All knew they had seen a record breaking eel and, to a degree, its loss took the edge off the rest of the day. It was certainly the largest eel I have ever seen or hooked, and to my mind the only good thing about the episode was that the fish had broken free completely: no hook in its jaw, no trace or line dragging until it finally snagged onto some obstruction, leaving the giant eel to die tethered to the remains of a rusting first war relic.

Large as this eel was, it is still small fry when compared to many wreck eels. Most charter boat skippers can tell you of monster eels hooked and lost, several thought to weigh over 150 pounds. Such eels still exist on most wrecks but, so far, nobody has managed to bring one to the gaff.

One day a really, really large eel will be taken and a new record for the species will be established. When this does occur, and it undoubtedly will happen, that record may stand for all time, for a giant conger is one of the most difficult of all fish to catch.

Other Big Game Fishing

Barracuda

The European barracuda is on average far smaller than its tropical counterpart. The European fish are taken mainly in waters around all three sets of Atlantic islands, that is, the Azores, Canaries and Madeira.

Although the fish weigh less than ten pounds on average they can grow to double this figure. I knew this last point for a fact, for a 21½ pound specimen I caught from the Formigas Rocks in the Azores is at present awaiting ratification as the new European record.

Formigas Rocks (ant rocks) lie approximately 70 miles out from the island of San Miguel. From a big game fishing point of view the rocks are an angler's paradise. Rich in sea life and capable of producing dozens of different species of fish. The usual way of fishing off Formigas is to stay overnight on the boat, fishing or sleeping as you wish.

On this occasion, when I caught the possible record barracuda, we had arrived on the Tuesday morning, fished very successfully until dusk, then grabbed a few hours of well-earned sleep before resuming our fishing at dawn. The plan was to leave at midday on Wednesday and arrive back at Porta Delgada in time to get an evening meal. Fish were in plentiful supply, particularly bermuda chub of up to 11½ pounds in weight. These very game fish were taken on tiny spinning rods and light line, and gave us unbelievable sport. The final part of our plan was to troll around the rocks, take a few barracuda then troll back to home base. Small barracuda were plentiful and in an attempt to find a larger fish, I decided to try trolling a large Kona Head lure which incorporated a yellow rubber skirt, barracuda seem unable to resist lures which incorporate yellow. I hoped that a bait of this colour would tempt an outsize specimen to attack. Having mounted the lure, I let it run out behind the boat and as I pushed forward the gear lever of my reel I distinctly saw a broad bar of silver sweep up and engulf the lure.

Barracuda invariably hook themselves and this fish was no exception. The odd thing about barracuda is that – even on light tackle – they seldom put up much of a battle. Unfortunately, this fish was also well out-gunned by the 30 pound class outfit I was using, and after a couple of short ineffectual runs it allowed itself to be led alongside the boat and gaffed without a struggle.

The real trick to good, enjoyable barracuda fishing is to use a rod of the 12 pound class which will allow barracuda to put up a better fight. On the occasion I caught this fish I did not have a rod of that light calibre with me otherwise the battle might have been more equal. Barracuda offer good sport to the angler who does not want to tangle with giant shark, marlin or tuna, and as a European game species they are high on the list of target fish.

Dorado

The dorado (a dolphin) is one of the most beautiful of all sea creatures. The colours of a live specimen are far too beautiful to describe accurately, and unfortunately they soon fade as the fish expires.

From a sport fisherman's point of view the dorado is a great game fish to catch on light tackle. Dorado (fish of gold) seldom reach a weight of more than 30 pounds in European waters. Because of this, I like to fish an outfit of 12 or 20 pound class. The 12 pound class tackle is the best, for it allows the dorado to put up a magnificent battle: a struggle which often includes a dazzling display of aerobatics. Dorado are shoal fish which prey actively on small surface-dwelling bait fish such as mackerel and flying fish. Often encountered by the hundred, dorado can be found round all the Atlantic Islands.

My favourite method for taking dorado is to troll for them using a red-gill sand eel. They will also take natural baits, plug baits and flashy metal spoon-type lures. However, the red-gill with its frantically waggling tail and soft rubbery body seems to attract and catch more dorado than any other type of lure I have used.

The trick to dorado fishing is to locate a shoal, for once such a shoal is located the fish will come thick and fast. I remember once fishing off Madeira with two other anglers when no fewer than 49 fine dorado were caught. I was the only one fishing red-gill and I boated no less than 42 of the fish taken. So deadly was the red-gill that day, that on several occasions when a fish was hooked and then managed to shake off the hook, a second fish would charge the red-gill and snatch it.

Once on a feeding spree dorado are 'kill-crazy' as this particular day proved. The knack of locating dorado is a simple one. If a raft or mat of floating weed or debris can be located, then you can be sure that dorado will not be far away. And often they will be right under the weed, taking full advantage of the shade given by the raft. The bait should be trolled past, as close as possible to the debris, and if fish are present the bait will be taken instantly.

For this sort of fishing I like to use a long trace and a special trolling lead to keep the lure down just beneath the surface (see

Fig. 25). Wire traces are not advisable for dorado fishing, although the trace should be made up from nylon of heavier breaking strain than the reel line. I use nylon of a 25 pound

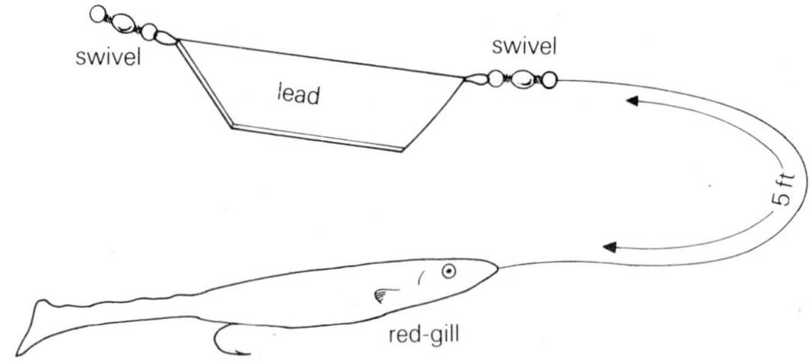

FIGURE 25   The most deadly lure for dorado is a red-gill (a plastic or rubber sand eel) fished on a long trace with a special trolling lead to keep the red-gill just below the surface.

breaking strain for all my dorado traces and have never lost a fish as a result.

For the big game angler who likes to bottom fish, the grouper (or meron) offers a perfect target. This giant fish often reaches weights in excess of 80 pounds and is most often caught in comparatively shallow water close to the land.

Grouper like to live close to rocks and reefs, where they normally take up permanent residence in underwater caves or overhangs. Once again the volcanic islands of Madeira, Azores and the Canary Islands offer the perfect habitat for these huge fish.

Light tackle is of no value where these fish are concerned, as a grouper seldom ventures more than a yard or two from cover and once hooked makes an instant rush for its stronghold. Once undercover, a grouper is extremely difficult to dislodge, and for this reason heavy tackle is essential. The perfect tackle for the job is an 80 pound class rod with reel to match. Because of the rugged habitat preferred by the grouper, nylon line should be used in preference to dacron. Traces should be wire with a 100 pound breaking strain, fitted with 10-0 or 12-0 hooks of the Mustad Seamaster type.

Grouper have huge mouths and show a marked preference for big baits. My own experience leads me to believe that oily-fleshed fish – like mackerel or bonito – makes the best grouper bait. Grouper obviously hunt by smell rather than sight, and the smell trail left by an oily bait definitely helps to attract fish.

My favourite bait is a half-fresh bonito, and it was on this bait that I took a 70 pound grouper on my last visit to Madeira. A local boatman had told me that he knew of a place which held some huge specimens and I agreed to fish for them on the following day. It was June and the weather was beautiful. The area I was to fish was nearly three hours from Funchal Harbour, and to while away time on the long trip I put out two trolling rods to try for bonito and barracuda. The fishing was not too good during the journey out but I did manage to catch one nice bonito weighing around 6 pounds, plus several European barracuda of similar size.

The fishing grounds when we reached them were directly beneath the cliffs and Porta Da Sol (point of the sun) where the bottom was clearly visible through the glass clear water. By visible I mean that below us great slabs of volcanic rock could clearly be seen and between these ridges were dark canyons of unknown depth: it was into one of these canyons that I intended to drop my bait.

With only one bonito available I cut down on bait size, slicing the fish into three equal parts. I find the head section of a bonito to be the most effective, as the seepage of blood from the gill lays a thick scent trail that is perfect for luring a grouper out of its hole.

With the boat now neatly placed I was in a perfect position to drop my bait straight into a canyon, where, with luck, a big grouper would be in residence. I could actually watch as my bait dropped into the gully, and I judged the depth of the gully to be somewhere over 60 feet. My only fear was that the canyon might be infested with hefty moray eels which would take and ruin baits before a grouper came on the scene. Nothing happened for nearly an hour, then the rod twitched a couple of times and slowly started to pull down. This sort of bite is so deliberate that striking is simply a matter of raising the rod tip.

To get maximum leverage I stood up, set the hook and began to crank the reel handle, my hope was to lift the fish out of the gully but I did not succeed. The grouper started to move, slowly picking up speed as it went, and then seconds later all movement ceased and everything went solid. The fish had obviously got back to its home cave, where it was now firmly entrenched.

Under these circumstances an angler can either pull for a break, or else sit tight and hope the fish will assume danger has passed and come out to resume feeding. I waited for nearly 15 minutes before feeling any sort of movement. At first it seemed little to get excited about, not much more than a tiny vibration that set the rod tip trembling. Then my taut line began to fall slack and I knew the grouper was moving out of its lair. At this stage, my timing had to be perfect: if I tried to force the fish up too soon it would dive for cover, and if I left matters too long the grouper would almost certainly snag the trailing line on some obstruction.

The second I felt the time was right, I heaved on the rod tip and began to pump and lift the fish out of the canyon. Everything went well, and I clearly saw the huge brown fish shoot up out of the blackness of the gully and make its first run across the rock. A big grouper can show a surprising turn of speed and this fish was broad enough in the tail to pile on the pressure. Fortunately its run angled up from the rock, allowing me to gain quite a bit of additional line.

Twice it tried to get back into the canyon but, on each occasion, I was able to increase rod pressure and keep the grouper from its objective. Finally it rolled up on its side, ready for gaffing.

It was weighed in at the fish dock at Funchal some hours later at an ounce over 70 pounds. When first caught it may well have been over 80 pounds but dehydration and loss of blood from the gaff puncture had a caused a considerable weight loss. Grouper may not be every angler's dream fish but they are big and strong, and they provide good sport even on heavy tackle.

Compared to the ugly moray eel, the average conger is a pleasant peaceful sort of fish. There have recently been a number of programmes on British television which purport to show that the sharp toothed, snake like moray is a much maligned creature, happy to take scraps of fish from a diver's hand. Eels that do this have, I believe, been carefully fed over a long period of time. In the wild state, the moray is an evil tempered, highly dangerous fish which has all the charm and appeal of a man-eating tiger.

I do not write this lightly. Large moray are comparatively common in the Azores, Madeira and the Canary Islands. They are also highly feared by the experienced commercial fishermen. Even fishermen who are happy to tackle a mako or a great white shark fear the moray at all times.

Morays are similar in their habit to conger: they live mainly by catching live fish, but are happy to eat fresh dead fish and they live in caves and fissures in the rocks. Moray grow to weights in excess of 60 pounds in European waters, and come in a wide variety of colours. The commonest and largest species seem to be the brown and yellow variety. They are all strong fighters, and should be fished for with tackle in the 50 or 80 pound class.

Wire traces are essential to avoid constant breakages, for even a small moray has a formidable set of teeth. I have caught moray off most of the Atlantic Islands but the largest specimens I have ever encountered have been from around the Azores, and Fayal Island is particularly noted for producing large moray eels.

I remember on one occasion while living in the Azores that a friend of mine – a bank manager – from England came out on a three week visit. The man in question, Peter Kelly, is an avid angler with a long string of giant Irish skate and Orcadian halibut to his name. This was Peter's first visit to the Azores and he arrived equipped with a vast pile of rods and tackle.

On his first day we went out to a mark known as Porta da Isla (point of the island), where the water is around 240 feet deep and the bottom made up of volcanic rock. This point can be guaranteed to provide good fishing for a wide variety of fish, and I knew that Peter would catch plenty.

Initially we fished light, for various rock fish which we intended to use as bait. We filled a fish box with mixed fish within ten minutes and then started to prepare the heavy tackle. I baited Peter's hook with a comber (known locally as a garuper) and within a few minutes he had hooked and boated a 54 pound tope. A good start, but even better things were to come. On his second drop he had a savage take, and after a fierce 15 minute struggle raised a huge hammerhead shark to the surface. We had no use for the fish, so rather than kill it unnecessarily it was brought alongside and the trace cut with a pair of pliers.

Nothing more occurred for nearly an hour, and I was just thinking of asking the boat captain to move when Peter announced that he had a touch. Sure enough, as I watched his rod tip I could see that far below something was pulling lightly at the bait. The bite was so light I suspected that a small fish or squid was responsible. Several minutes later the rod tip was still twitching and the bite had still not begun to develop. By now I was convinced that a small squid was the culprit and I suggested that Peter reel up and change baits, as squid make an awful mess of a bait, shredding it out of all reason.

Peter duly lifted his rod and began to wind up line whereupon the 'squid' abruptly turned into something strong and highly aggressive. Whatever it was, it did not take kindly to finding itself on a large and very sharp hook, nor was it impressed by English Bank Managers on holiday! It made no attempt to seek sanctuary in the sunken rocks, instead it rose from the bottom and began to swim off rapidly.

Fortunately Peter was using heavy tackle and was able to apply enough pressure to force the fish upwards. All the same, the fight style of the fish was strange: it fought in tight circles continuously shaking its head, which in turn caused the well bent rod to jag sharply downwards. The mystery was soon solved. At sixty or so feet down it looked like little more than a brown blob in the clear water, but as it rose I could see clearly that it was a moray eel.

This was not an average specimen, it was big. Huge, brown and yellow as are all large moray, it looked more like a giant snake than a fish and it hit surface in a smoking cauldron of coils that made it seem even more snake like.

The captain gaffed it, at which point it turned its head and chewed large lumps out of the gaff handle. When this failed, it threw a body coil round the wood and reared up the handle, intending to climb right into the boat. The skipper did not hesitate. He dropped the gaff and eel, reached for a knife and cut the monster free of the line. Within seconds it was off the gaff and diving at speed for its rocky retreat. None of us cared. Moray eels may be big and they may be strong but I for one do not care for them in the boat.

One of the most exciting fish to emerge on the European scene in recent years in the wahoo. A long, lean firebrand of a fish which looked like a cross between a mackerel and a barracuda.

Basically an inshore species, the wahoo is found in both Madeira and the Canary Islands. Madeiran wahoo run larger than those caught in the Canary Islands, but unfortunately they are a very localised species, occurring only off Porta Da Sol. The Portuguese name for the wahoo is *cavara da India* (Indian mackerel) and for many years it was the mainstay catch of just one village on Madeira, Paulo Do Mar.

A surface feeder, the wahoo is normally found over reefs or similar outcrops where it is an active predator. Wahoo can be caught on livebait or on trolled natural or artificial baits. The wahoo is one of the fastest of all game fish, providing incredible sport when fished on lightish tackle. For most wahoo fishing, tackle of the 30 pound class will suffice, although 50 pound class tackle should be used when exceptionally large fish are expected.

The wahoo relies on its speed to get out of trouble when hooked. It will make long searing runs of a 100 yards or more, and will fight to the bitter end in its attempt to escape. Wahoo run to around 100 pounds in weight in Madeiran waters. This is large for the species, and the Madeiran average tends to be higher than in other wahoo areas. In the West Indies where wahoo average 40 pounds in weight an 80 pounder can be classed as a big fish. While in European waters a wahoo of 80 pounds is regarded as a good but not outstanding catch.

I was lucky enough to be one of the first anglers to take wahoo off Madeira. For many years I had heard that such fish existed but, to be honest, I was sceptical of the reports. To begin with, I had never seen wahoo brought into the Funchal fish market and assumed from this, as a species, wahoo simply did not exist in Madeiran waters. What I had not taken into account was that it was just the village of Paulo Do Mar that fished wahoo and, as this village was not accessible by boat at that time, all fish caught were disposed of locally.

Finally, however, the rumours became so persistent that I decided to hire a local boat and go and try for a fish or two. I already had plenty of wahoo experience from my fishing in the Bahamas and Mexico and I knew just what sort of bait to use: fresh mackerel mounted on a two hook rig (see Fig. 26). I always use the two hook tackle, for wahoo are highly adept at chopping baits off directly behind a hook. My theory when developing this was that if I did get a wahoo to strike I wanted to put it in the boat! The upshot of all this was that I caught five wahoo, up to 75 pounds in weight, with the largest fish being the first one caught.

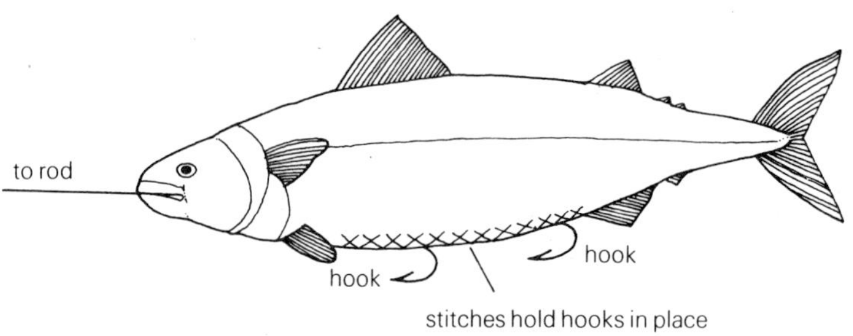

FIGURE 26   A fish mounted on a two hook rig is necessary bait for wahoo, as these fish are adept at biting short and chopping baits off directly behind a single hook.

The water on the fishing grounds was gin clear and soon after starting to troll I sighted a batch of about ten good-sized fish passing astern, these were the wahoo. Seconds after sighting the fish my bait was taken in typically explosive wahoo style. A wahoo strikes like a 6-inch shell hitting the water: a sort of muffled explosion that leaves a roll of white water to mark the point where the bait was taken. I was using 30 pound class tackle and the fish took off like a runaway train causing my reel to smoke and complain as the line was torn from it.

A big wahoo cannot be rushed on 30 pound tackle. Just when you feel the fish is on the verge of giving in, it will turn and start a run that you think will never end. At the end of the day and with five good, hard-fighting game fish in the boat, I really knew I had been fishing.

This then was the start of wahoo fishing off Madeira and possibly the first time wahoo had been taken on rod and line from European waters.

Since that first day wahoo have become an established European species. For the big game angler wishing to fish with comparatively light tackle, the wahoo is a species which offers immense possibilities and great excitement, and that is the basis of all good big game fishing.

Index

Numbers in *italic* refer to illustrations.